"I am to God
as a wave is to the ocean."

— Neale Donald Walsch

FAITHFULLY RELIGIONLESS

By Timber Hawkeye

HAWKEYE PUBLISHERS
HawkeyePublishers.com

Paperback ISBN	978-09858369-55
Hardcover ISBN	978-09858369-24
Ebook ISBN	978-09858369-48
Large Print ISBN	978-09858369-79

Also available in audio from audible.com and iTunes, narrated by Timber Hawkeye.

DeEtte,

This book is dedicated to you.

Discover the beauty of letting go!

The only thing I know

for certain is

that I don't know

anything for certain.

So I never argue with

anyone about anything.

I listen.

Life Journey

The past

doesn't define me,

it guides me.

I'm not a victim,

I'm a student.

I choose who I become

from this moment forward.

— 1 —

CULTURE SHOCK

It was a foggy Saturday morning in San Francisco, December 1st, 1990. My parents and sister were out of the house, and I was reading alone at the kitchen table. Around ten o'clock I noticed the family across the street drive away in their blue Jeep. The mom, dad, and two-daughter team returned home just a couple of hours later, but now they had a dead tree tied to the roof of their car.

Well, the tree wasn't exactly dead as in brown without any leaves or anything like that; it was actually very green and lush. But the tree's trunk had been sawed off, so there was no way it could be re-planted or revived. Stranger still, the neighbors didn't carry the tree through the side gate to their back yard (where one would expect a five-foot tree to go), they hauled it up the stairs and into the living room! They opened the curtains and positioned the tree by the window for everyone to see. What in the world were they doing?

Mesmerized, I put the book down and watched as they proceeded to wrap the tree with string lights and crown it with what looked like a Barbie doll at the very top. Like some perfectly-timed prank, our next-door neighbors pulled into their driveway with an identical tree in the back of their truck, and then a station wagon drove past our house with a similar tree sticking out the back.

I had never heard about Christmas before because five months prior to this phenomenon my family and I immigrated to the United States from Israel, where I was born and raised until my early teens.

It wouldn't be fair to say that I was raised Jewish, however. My family never kept kosher (a longstanding Jewish practice that outlaws the simultaneous consumption of dairy and meat, for example, as well as prohibiting certain seafood dishes, pork, and a few other technicalities); nor did we ever celebrate any of the Jewish holidays (or any holiday, for that matter). We only went to the synagogue once a year, and even that was more of a social tradition than a devotional one. And although I had studied the Old Testament at school because it was as mandatory as geography and math, it was more of a history class than a cultural one (except we didn't learn about any other religions). According to Jewish law, Judaism is a religion that is assigned to you at birth (if your mother is Jewish then so are you, whether you acknowledge it or not).

We never discussed God at home, and the one time I asked my dad about the questionable Bible stories I was learning at school, he simply told me not to take them too seriously.

One of the first things I noticed when I moved to the States, however, was that people in America were significantly more in touch with their religion than anyone I had met in Israel.

It was interesting to observe my extended family in California clinging to their Judaism as something that unites them, while I was more curious in exploring the diversity around me (especially after the Christmas tree incident).

There were many new religions for me to discover, and very little of what I initially witnessed made any sense. It turns out Christmas trees have nothing to do with Christ, and although Easter is about Jesus' resurrection, the holiday focuses mainly on the Easter Bunny, who only appears cute and cuddly but apparently judges children as either good or disobedient. There was so much to learn!

I started thinking about my own beliefs and philosophies, where and how they had originated, and whether they had any merit or validity. It became clear that I had somehow constructed my own belief system, but I had never taken the time to question it.

As it turned out, some of my own beliefs didn't even make sense: I still experienced a moment of trepidation whenever I accidentally dropped the saltshaker at a restaurant or crossed a black cat on the street. Am I forever doomed? Or did tossing salt over my left shoulder fix everything?

We've all been raised to believe more superstitions than we realize. And over the years, we have either written them off as nothing more than folklore, or we actually accept them as true and then call them beliefs, not superstitions.

As children, we rarely demand evidence for anything we are taught. Like sponges, we simply soak everything up. For example, I remember teachers telling a group of students at my school that if anyone were to step over us while we sat on the floor, it would forever stunt our growth (unless, of course, they immediately step back the way they had come). This superstition was the teachers' seemingly innocent effort to prevent anyone from tripping over the students who sat in the hallways with their legs stretched out, but I still question their methods of preying on our vulnerability and gullibility. We not only obediently sat with our legs crossed after that, we also fervently warned all the other students of the terrible fate awaiting them if they weren't careful to do the same.

The concept of scaring people into compliance is nothing new, of course; it's biblical. But scare-tactics greatly underestimate our reasoning intelligence. As Albert Einstein surmised, "If people are only good because they fear punishment or hope for reward, then we are a sorry lot indeed!"

And so we get older, but the superstitions don't stop. A four-leaf clover is a sign of good luck (just like a rabbit's foot or a horseshoe), but heaven forbid we open an umbrella indoors or walk under a ladder, right? If you hear ringing in your left ear, it's apparently because someone is speaking ill of you (whereas the opposite is true with the right). And if your palm itches, it supposedly means you will receive a large sum of money from an unexpected source. So go ahead... scratch that palm just in case; it's no different than knocking on wood to avoid bad luck.

At some point, however, we stop believing that a watermelon would actually grow in our stomachs if we were to accidentally swallow a seed (just like we stop believing in Santa Claus or the Tooth Fairy). Yet 85% of skyscrapers still skip the 13th floor, and we continue to wish on shooting stars and birthday candles.

By setting out to understand what people believe, why we believe what we do, and how much of what we believe is actually true, I've learned that all of our truths (individual or collective) depend on time, place, and circumstance.

The black cat, for instance, is a symbol of prosperity and good luck in Scotland and Japan, but it's a symbol of misfortune and even death in most European and Western cultures. What is true for one person isn't necessarily true for another. But what if the cat is just a cat (neither good nor evil), and we are just compulsive, Meaning-Making Machines who assign reason to whatever we don't understand?

My conclusion is that the only thing that makes something true is our choice to believe that it is. Some may argue that things like gravity are true whether we choose to believe in them or not, but even gravity is subject to time, place, and circumstance; travel far enough away from the center of the earth, or dive into water, and the effects of gravity start to change.

We search for answers, come up with theories, and even make up stories, all in an effort to explain the unexplainable. We are so afraid of not knowing the truth, in fact, that we prefer believing a lie rather than living with the discomfort of the unknown.

But this book doesn't intend to disprove anyone's beliefs; I assure you. I actually rejoice in the beauty of mystery because a great calm and inner peace can be derived from letting go of our compulsive need to know.

I don't consider myself a skeptic, nor do I claim that the world is full of lies. On the contrary: I believe the world is full of truths.

Whether it's astrology, romance, destiny, Christ, Muhammad, Judaism, anarchy, heaven, or any other story or theory that we've ever heard, what makes them true is our choice to believe that they are. And for the most part, that's okay.

Everything is a belief system (whether it's ancient or new, dogmatic or otherwise). Beliefs are based on personal choices and experiences, often founded on subjective feelings. It is therefore inevitable that the exact opposite of what each of us knows to be true is equally true for somebody else, somewhere else, depending on their time, place, or circumstance.

Having faith, however, is not about knowing anything with absolute certainty, but about being okay (even relieved) that some things cannot be known. When we didn't know what caused thunder and lightening, for example, we believed God was expressing anger and disapproval. But that's not faith, that's scapegoating.

We can't know why certain things occur, but faith in God acknowledges that God works in mysterious ways for reasons far beyond our comprehension. This does not necessarily translate to believing in organized religion, the Bible, or, least of all, the church. I use the word "God," by the way, to encompass all variations of mystery; be it the Universe, Higher Power, Mother Nature, Father Time, Energy, etc. My definition of God doesn't conjure a white, bearded man in the sky who dispenses blessings for good behavior and harsh judgments to condemn the bad. That's because I don't believe God does that; religion does. And as Anne Lamott cleverly put it, "You can safely assume you've created God in your own image if it turns out that your God hates the same people you do."

Our sensitive egos turn personal opinions into what we often mistakenly call "facts," but they aren't factual at all; just comforting. And that's where mindful discretion is imperative to distinguish between beliefs that the ego clings to for validation, and unbiased observations that focus on what is really going on (inconvenient and uncomfortable as they may be).

If we're lucky, we find something to believe in that contributes to our overall happiness, health, peace-of-mind, and sense of purpose. It doesn't matter whether we experience a deep connection with a higher power through prayer, meditation, nature, service, congregation, song, silence, movement, art, illness, or even a near-death incident; what matters is that we remember our moment of truth (unique to us as it may be); that we live in line with our core values (whatever they may be); and that we allow others to explore and experience the divine in whatever form resonates with them the most (even if it's completely different from our own, because different isn't wrong).

While I think having a belief system can be beneficial, it can be dangerous to believe in something solely because we have heard it repeated a million times or, worse yet, because we've repeated it to ourselves over the course of many years.

Growing up, one of my closest friends believed that she would never amount to anything, that she was unattractive, and that her ultimate failure was inevitable in whatever she pursued. None of this was true, of course, but because her father repeatedly said this to her from childhood through puberty, she ultimately (perhaps inevitably) accepted this as true. Even years after her father was no longer around, she continued telling people what a failure she was, and it didn't matter how many friends told her she was charming or beautiful because as long as she didn't believe it to be true, then it wasn't (at least not for her... not for many years).

So what is true? Is Lily beautiful or not? Well, she's technically neither beautiful nor not beautiful, but her experience in life is ultimately shaped and greatly affected by what she chooses to believe (as is the case with many of us). We can choose to believe that we are perfect by design, gifted, smart, capable, fortunate, blessed, and worthy; or we can choose to believe the opposite. It took Lily 36 years to change what she believed, but that's the wonderful news about reevaluating our belief system: we can embrace a new truth even after decades of believing the opposite. Or, of course, we can choose to stay stuck. Either way, we have to live with the consequences.

To accept a new truth, we must be willing to let go of an old one, and that's where most people struggle: ignoring or forgetting whatever society has previously deemed as beautiful, successful, saint-like, or heaven-bound, and redefining who we are according to new and improved standards.

In my continued efforts to articulate the beauty of faith while delicately explaining the potential danger of organized religion, I've learned that while one person may consider something to be crucial and absolutely true, another person can consider that very same truth to be completely irrelevant. And while spirituality affords us the flexibility to be okay with that dichotomy, organized religion not only attempts to dictate a pre-packaged belief system as universally applicable, it does so with such unwavering disregard for time, place, or circumstance, that it's downright inconsiderate at best, and cruel or criminal at worst. Don't get me wrong: religion can be extremely comforting, but having faith in God (any God) and putting one's faith in organized religion, are two very different things.

To put it another way: faith is a spiritual practice of continually letting go of certainty, of ego, and of the underlying need to know, while religion is a traditional, ceremonial clinging to concrete dogmas, stubborn rigidity, and ageless rituals. One is love-based, liberated, and free, while the other is fear-based, confined, and restricted. As Robert Oxton Bolton said, "A belief is not merely an idea that the mind possesses, it is an idea that possesses the mind."

There is danger in blindly accepting something as true just for the sake of believing in something: un-learning an idea is significantly more difficult than picking it up in the first place. As Rumi said, "The art of knowing is knowing what to ignore." And the longer we cling to our beliefs, the harder it gets to let them go (even when presented with evidence to the contrary).

The beauty of finding our own truth is that there is no need to convince other people of it, nor any reason to nullify someone else's reality in order to validate our own. If someone were to tell me that the sky is green, for example, and I believe it to be blue, I see no need to tell them they are wrong, nor do I need to feel superior by making them inferior. I simply walk away from that experience with the newfound knowledge that to some people the sky looks green... and that's okay. Maybe that person is color blind, or maybe they've seen the Northern Lights or the sky before a thunderstorm. Regardless of their reasons, the blueness of my sky is not threatened nor jeopardized by how green someone else perceives it to be.

Any urge that a person feels to push their personal opinions onto others is either ego-driven or a result of their own insecurities. In Yogananda's Autobiography of a Yogi, this is referred to as "Feeling tall by cutting off the heads of other men." Surely there's a healthier way to boost our confidence without trying to destroy someone else's (at least that's what my dad taught me).

Without even intending to do it, just through his continued honesty and open-mindedness about religion and politics, my father raised me to understand that there is absolutely no harm in listening to whatever anyone has to say, but to take it all with a grain of salt. And by forming and expressing his own opinions (often different from societal norms), he again encouraged me to pursue my curiosity in order to arrive at my own conclusions. Isn't it funny how we can learn so much more from watching our parents' behavior than from anything they actually try to teach us? I wish all children could be taught HOW to think instead of WHAT to think.

When I tell people that I don't have a religion, they automatically assume I don't believe in God; but nothing could be further from the truth. Consider this book my personal train of thought, making random stops along the way, and offering reflections of my own journey from having "faithless religion" to being "faithfully religionless." I'm not against any religion; I simply don't have one, nor do I believe we need it to be ethical. As Gerry Spence brilliantly summarized, "It is better to have a mind opened by wonder, than a mind closed by belief."

You decide
for how long
you're going to let
what hurt you
haunt you.

— 2 —

RESILIENCE

The Israel I see portrayed in the media is nothing like the Israel in which I grew up. I was born and raised in a tiny little town in the Golan Heights (the northern most part of the country), where everyone was white, Jewish, and identical to me. Despite what images on television might have you believe, I did not dodge bullets on my way to school, and the word "Arab" wasn't synonymous with "enemy;" it was just an adjective for delicious food and great music.

In fact, even with frequent visits to my grandmother's place in Tel Aviv (three hours south of my hometown), I didn't get to meet anyone who was Arab until moved to America in the early 90's. We did not live in the desert, and I didn't ride a camel to school (though it sounds like fun, now that I think about it).

The main street that cut across my hometown was lined with palm trees in the middle and olive trees on the sides. I still remember my dad sending me out with a large bucket to pick green olives, which he would later cure in brine for a few months. The streets had foot traffic at all hours of the day and night. We never had a curfew, and we never locked our front door because we had nothing to fear.

When I tell Americans that our school parties took place at underground bomb shelters located throughout the city, it sounds foreign and absurd, maybe even scary. But growing up there and never having to use those bomb shelters for any purpose other than to hang a disco ball and dance to Cyndi Lauper, Madonna, and Michael Jackson, there was nothing scary about the space; it's where I held hands with a girl and practiced kissing for the first time.

Like most European kids in the eighties, we grew up playing ball outdoors when the weather was nice, then switched to video games on the Commodore 64 when it wasn't. We watched one of the three television channels that were available in Israel at the time: a station out of Lebanon to the north broadcasting shows like Dynasty (which was an American series); another station out of Jordan to the east showed the Smurfs (who were Belgian but spoke Arabic with Hebrew subtitles so that we could understand what they were saying); and, of course, a local Israeli station on which we watched Sesame Street, featuring Kippi Ben Kipod (who was a large porcupine) instead of Big Bird (don't ask).

The Israeli channel covered the news and current events every hour on the hour. And, not to sound cold or insensitive, but on the rare occasions when news broke out about a terrorist who bombed a bus in one of the major cities, life didn't stop; people just caught the next bus or opted to walk instead. You see, despite being surrounded by acts of terrorism, we refused to be terrorized. We essentially grew up learning that painful realities are better off accepted because our reaction to events can often be more damaging than the events themselves.

In Buddhism, this resilience is encapsulated as "Pain is inevitable, but suffering is optional." Whether we're talking about pain in the form of old age, sickness, death, or any type of loss or trauma, the pain itself is inevitable, but our prolonged suffering from that pain is completely optional (it's the one and only part of the equation we can actually control by learning to keep our minds at peace).

Exposure to this level of composure from a very early age has played a tremendous role in shaping my world-view. If Israelis and Palestinians can choose not to be terrorized in the face of terror, then the problem in our day-to-day lives is not other people who are irritating, for example, but the fact that we are so susceptible to irritation. And since we can't control what other people do, the only thing we can work on is maintaining internal peace in the face of external conflict.

This perspective has given me the ability to not get stressed or frustrated even in the midst of frustrating or stressful situations. We all face harsh realities in life, but we can do so without letting the situations' severity disturb our serenity.

This reminds me of when an audience member asked the Dalai Lama why he didn't fight back against the Chinese. He simply smiled and said, "Of course the mind can rationalize fighting back, but the heart would never understand. Then you would be divided in yourself, the heart and the mind, and the war would be inside you."

Even with the occasional attacks in the news, growing up in Israel was not very different from life here in the United States, where violence is actually significantly more rampant with all the high school shootings, church fires, and riots. One could argue that residents of the Middle East are actually better prepared to deal with tragedy without being traumatized precisely because of all those years of resilience.

Just like water from the ocean won't sink a boat unless the water gets inside the boat, the negativity of the world can't bring me down unless I allow it to get inside. This is not to be mistaken with sticking my head in the sand in order to avoid seeing the injustices in the world; my eyes are actually wide open, which is why I can see all of the beauty in the world as well (I'm not blinded by the veil of doom).

So despite waking up every day and hearing the radio newscaster detail how many crimes were committed the night before, I still headed off to school, both my parents went to work (dad was a mechanic, mom was a kindergarten teacher), and our daily flow of life was not disrupted so long as we didn't allow it to be.

My dad had been fixing cars since he was 14 years old. He hated his job and told me that if I ever consider following his footsteps, he would cut off both my arms to make sure I can't. Needless to say, as impressed as I am today by exquisite car design and technology, I have no idea what goes on under the hood, and my dad couldn't be happier about it.

Six years before we moved from Israel to the States, a unique factory opened in our small town. It packaged pasteurized cows' milk into cartons similar to what we now see almond, soy, or rice milk packaged into, with no need for refrigeration until it is opened (a product that is still available across Europe today, but not in the United States). That's when my dad caught his lucky break from being a car mechanic and started working in the factory.

He often took me to work with him to meet his coworkers, to witness the magic of assembly line production, and to see him smile (something he never did in the auto shop and rarely ever did at home).

My dad's work schedule had him leaving for the factory before I woke up each morning and returning home after I had already gone to bed, so we rarely got to spend any quality time together. During the rare instances when we did, however, I clung to every word of wisdom he imparted, and I learned even more from simply observing him interact with others.

He was in his mid-thirties when we moved to the United States, and his inability to speak English didn't prevent him from finding work because he was fluent in the universal language of car engines. Reluctantly, he got a job at one garage after another, until he was finally able to run his own shop when he turned 50. It didn't make him dread working on cars any less, but as part-owner he could at least delegate the more physically demanding aspects of the job to the younger employees.

It was one thing for him to hate his job when he was younger, but getting a break from it during the six years that he worked at the factory and then having to return to the same profession that he'd sworn off was even harder. Any semblance of a spark in my dad's eyes was completely gone, imparting yet another valuable lesson without saying a word: that nothing is worth it if you aren't happy.

Whenever I'm dumped

or fired, laid off or

brushed off, I'm not being

rejected, I'm being

re-directed.

And I'm grateful for

it all.

— 3 —

MIND TRICKS

My parents took me to an aquarium when I was really young (at least that's what they tell me). I don't recall the trip, so how can I know for sure that it ever took place? If my parents have lied about other things in the past (and they have), then there is no way for me to know whether the trip to the aquarium was real or made up.

Despite this uncertainty, my peace of mind comes from letting go of the need to know. It's not that I don't care (carelessness is harsh). I have simply accepted that among other things in life, this will forever remain a mystery, and I'm perfectly okay with that.

"Don't believe everything you think!" is probably the best advice I've ever been given. Our thoughts are rarely ever truly our own; they are shaped by the people around us or by current events and media exposure. Even when we think of something ourselves (or we think we do), it's important to remember that the mind is strangely capable of believing just about anything in order to avoid internal conflict and dissonance.

If you tell somebody a good story, they are going to believe it. The story doesn't have to be true to be believable; it simply has to be good enough. And the same is true of the stories we tell ourselves.

By conveniently overlooking what would otherwise be an obvious deterrent, we repeatedly talk ourselves into believing that something is a "good idea." Whether we convince ourselves that buying a car we clearly can't afford is a smart choice, or we talk ourselves into dating someone with "trouble" written all over them simply because they're attractive, we basically lie to ourselves on a regular basis, which is why it's best not to believe everything we think.

So what's left? If we're to take everything that other people tell us with a grain of salt (including the books we read, or the news we hear), and we can't even trust our own thoughts, then what can we believe? Our feelings? Definitely not! Feelings are valid, but they aren't facts. They also change at the drop of a dime and can frequently be flat-out wrong! All too often I have felt like someone was mad at me, for example, and then it turned out that they weren't. I have felt overweight when I really wasn't, and I still sometimes feel like I'm incapable of doing something until the very moment it is actually done. So if thoughts are to be taken with a grain of salt, then feelings ought to be served with a spoonful!

Whenever we feel inadequate, therefore, it's best to catch ourselves in our own lie and set the record straight: we are actually capable, strong, beautiful, and incredibly blessed. All the other negative self-talk is commentary by a troll in our own minds with nothing better to do than bully us.

Since our thoughts can't be trusted and what other people tell us is always biased, and even our feelings aren't facts, then our personal experience is the only thing we can truly trust. There is an ancient Chinese proverb that says, "I hear and I forget. I see and I remember. But when I do, I understand!" We never have to be convinced of something that we have experienced first hand. The challenge, however, is to differentiate between our actual experience and the memories, thoughts, and/or feelings we have about it (because the experience itself is the only thing we can trust; everything else is questionable).

This line of thinking would be even more intriguing if my parents had a photograph of me at the aquarium, which would prove that I was there regardless of whether or not I could recall the experience. Then I would know that it happened even though it made no impact on me whatsoever (either because I was too young to form any memories, or because even though I was physically there, I was mentally somewhere else).

So... if we can remain unaffected by something that actually happened, can we also be forever changed by something that never did? We can only conclude that our life experience is more significantly shaped by what goes on in our minds than what goes on with our bodies.

There is a scar on my forehead from when I cracked it open as a child. Depending on whom you ask, it is either the result of being beaten by my mom, or an innocent accident when we were goofing around. One explanation is traumatic, while the other is insignificant; but which is true? If you ask my mother, she would tell you we were playing when I accidentally slipped and fell, but if you ask me, I recall her chasing after me in a fit of rage to beat me up. I glanced back to see where she was, and when I turned around, I ran into the wall and cracked my forehead open.

When she physically abused us, was she being the best mother she knew to be (like her mother had been and her grandmother before that?), or was she committing a crime, which is what she would have certainly been accused of doing had it happened here in the U.S.?

I am more inclined to believe that according to my mother's truth, she wasn't doing anything wrong (who was it who said "Nobody ever does anything wrong given their model of the world?"). Forgiving her has nothing to do with agreeing that what she did was right, but simply accepting that it was right for her. This is how I can simultaneously forgive her and still maintain my own truth about how I got the scar. While there is only one fact about how the injury occurred, there are two separate truths about it (mine and hers). Facts and truths are very different things.

It was my college astronomy professor who helped me distinguish between "truth" and "facts." Science, he explained, is a search for facts, not for truth. It sets out to answer HOW things came into existence, for example, but it doesn't concern itself with WHY they came to be.

Religion, on the other hand, not only attempts to answer why things came to be, but subsequently calls its answers the "Truth" (with a capital "T," no less), often with absolutely no regard for conflicting facts.

Scientists can (and regularly do), make new discoveries that invalidate or append earlier data (even if it means admitting previous findings were shortsighted). This is possible because science has no emotional attachment to that information.

Organized religion, unfortunately, does not allow new discoveries to amend or append earlier statements. In fact, I don't think religion CAN do that, because pulling one string could potentially unravel the whole thing.

It's important to constantly reevaluate our beliefs and, if need be, let them go. What was true yesterday may not be true today. Some old beliefs are simply no longer applicable to our current time, place, or circumstance, and clinging to them would be like keeping an old pair of shoes that no longer fit.

Before I go any further, it's extremely important that I explain the difference between feelings and emotions. You'll quickly see why I embrace the full range of feelings that we experience throughout the day, yet endlessly bad-mouth emotions and their destructive nature.

In a nutshell, a feeling lasts somewhere between 45 seconds and a minute-and-a-half; that's all. We rarely notice the shift, but it is perfectly natural for us to be completely overcome by a certain feeling in one minute, only to experience another feeling a few minutes later (all without us being diagnosed as bipolar).

For example, somebody at the office says something that really upsets you, but then your favorite song comes on the radio and you're dancing in your seat. You are joyous and relieved when you get home from work, but upset again when you discover the dog relieved himself on the bedroom floor... Again. We jump from one feeling to another, and that is the natural course of feelings as they arise and dissipate from one moment to the next. Feelings are just like the thoughts in our minds, like clouds in the sky, or traffic on a busy street: they drift in and out of our field of awareness, sometimes spontaneous, sometimes learned, but always fleeting.

Emotions, on the other hand, are a completely different burden. They are the stories we construct around a feeling about what happened, as opposed to what actually took place, and we often dramatize, inflate, and blow them completely out of proportion. If there was an actual road to happiness, emotions would be the potholes on the otherwise smooth path toward euphoria.

Innocently enough, emotions start out as honest feelings, but then we construct a story around them, which is a momentary yet giant leap from "I love you" (a feeling, for example) to "I can't live without you" (an emotion). One is a feeling that can get stronger over time (as we can love someone anew every moment of every day), and the other is a lie that we tell ourselves and actually start believing as time goes on.

This is how and why people can stay angry with someone for a decade or two instead of only for a brief moment. The triggering event that initially angered us happened in the past, and the person who upset us may not even be in our lives anymore, but as long as we continue mulling over the experience, essentially re-living it in our minds and bodies, we will keep experiencing it and never fully recover. By believing, re-living, and repeating the elaborate story that we constructed around the initial feeling, we keep the emotion alive, and it burns inside of us for years to come. It feels very real to us, but it's only a memory of a feeling felt long ago. It's best to think of the memory of our pain as a scar, which will remind us of where we've been without dictating where we're going.

If, however, you insist on using your creative abilities to narrate every situation in your life, then why not use that creativity to your benefit? When somebody in a BMW cuts you off on the freeway, for example, and you create a story in your head that "all people in BMW's are jerks," then you won't simply be upset in that one moment, but every time you see a BMW in the future. I met a clever woman who told me that whenever somebody cuts her off, she just tells herself that they're speeding because they really have to pee. It's still just a story, mind you, and it's no truer than the other, but this story is lighthearted, helps her relate to the person who cut her off, and keeps her in a good mood!

Our tendency to react emotionally (be it on the freeway, at the office, or at home) is a learned habitual pattern. But with enough practice, we can rationally (instead of habitually), respond to the world around us. If the story you tell yourself puts you in a mood in which you don't want to be, simply catch the narrator in action and change the story.

A few years ago, during a guided group meditation exercise, we were asked to sit comfortably, close our eyes, and think back to the saddest moment in our lives. We were gently invited to recall who was with us at the time and what we were wearing (as well as the sounds, smells, and textures of that moment), all in an effort to remember the event with as much detail as possible. Whether we conjured up the memory of a death in the family, a recent heartbreak, divorce, or the loss of a pet, observing the group from the back of the room, you could clearly see everyone's posture slowly slouch with heavy shoulders, and a few people rocking back-and-forth as they started to cry. It was as if they weren't merely thinking about the experience but going through it all over again.

We were then asked to recall a happy time in our lives (be it the moment we fell in love, a surprise birthday party; or anything else from the past that makes us smile).

Although still sitting in silence with eyes closed, the shift in people's thoughts was clearly visible from the back of the room yet again. This time, everyone's posture straightened, smiles began to spread across their faces, and a few people even began to giggle as the memory took shape in their minds.

Much like before, it was as if they were not simply revisiting a memory, but going through the experience in real time. In my mind during that exercise, I went back to the beach in Hawaii, overjoyed by the smell of plumerias and the sound of crashing waves. Snapshots of local families gathered around a barbecue pit playing ukuleles immediately brought a smile to my face; that's my happy place; a sanctuary I can revisit without a plane ticket at any time.

The power behind that exercise was that we were in complete control of how we felt. I'm going to say it again: we were in complete control of how we felt!

As it turns out, we actually decide how to feel at any given moment. And yet how many times throughout our lives have we heard someone say, "I can't help the way I feel!" or, worse yet, "You make me feel _____."

When you think about it, "You make me feel" is a crazy thing to say; it literally blames someone else for our own thoughts!

Those statements ("I can't help the way I feel" and "You make me feel...") rob us of our inherent power and personal responsibility. The moment we say those words, we turn ourselves into victims, easily manipulated and controlled by others, instead of mature, accountable, calm and collected adults.

Emotions (and emotional reactivity) are at the root of what stirs our lives away from where we ultimately want to be. The good news is that we don't have to be slaves to our emotions; we can be in complete control over them (thereby in harmony with our lives). The bad news is that we've been playing the victim for so long that it can be difficult to regain control. As difficult as this may sound, however, taking the time and making the effort to learn how to control our minds is significantly easier in the long run than living the rest of our lives as victims; that's for sure.

The villain here, so to speak, is the emotional attachment that we develop to things, people, and beliefs. Attachment is not only extremely debilitating and restrictive, but a dangerously detrimental tendency if left unchecked. Love and life without attachment is a lost art in western culture, often criticized for being less passionate, even though it's actually more intense because it honors every fleeting moment without trying to stretch or bury it. Non-attachment allows us to fully experience everything unconditionally, without the very things that ruin our experience in the here and now: fear, regret, worry, and stress.

I'm not suggesting that it's unnatural for us to feel sad, angry, or overjoyed (it would actually be unnatural for us not to). I'm only questioning our habit to emote sadness, anger, frustration, etc., and whether it is beneficial or detrimental for us to do so. If nothing else, it's exhausting!

Eleanor Roosevelt said, "No one can make you feel inferior without your consent." And I not only agree with her, I firmly believe that no one can make us feel ANYTHING without our consent. In other words, no one can drive you crazy unless you give them the keys. ☺

The moment we make someone else responsible for our feelings is the moment we choose to be a victim. Meditation is beneficial because it exercises our ability to first observe and then control our own thoughts. We then develop the ability to CHOOSE to be happy. This ability is beautifully portrayed in the following story:

> Carol's husband died after a long battle with cancer. Carol's son didn't want her to live alone, so he invited her to move-in with him in Europe, and she joyfully accepted his invitation.
>
> He began to describe the house to her on the flight over, and she immediately said, "I love it!"
>
> "But you haven't even seen it yet," he laughed, "just wait!"
>
> "It doesn't matter!" Carol replied. "Happiness is something you choose ahead of time. How much I like the house has nothing to do with the exterior paint or the way you've arranged the furniture; it has everything to do with how I choose to look at it, and I have already decided to love it!"

Think about all the instances when you've set yourself up to dislike something before even trying it, or predicted your own failure before your first attempt (if any). I used to do this all the time.

I remember how I used to take offense whenever I felt religion was forced upon me, like the time I dated a nurse who worked at a hospital where a crucifix hung above every bed. I said unreasonable things like, "Even if I get into a car accident, you better not bring me here!" There was a time when I downright hated "Bible Pushers," but that was before I started thinking of them as no different than friends who discover a great restaurant that they say I "have to try!" These folks found something that brings them tremendous joy or peace of mind, and they simply want me to experience it too; what's so terrible about that? It's actually pretty sweet!

Now I'm happy for people and whatever religion they have found. A crucifix is no more offensive to me than any other work of art. Giving my opinions "a day off" is extremely liberating. My response to someone's recommendation of a religion or a restaurant is now the same: "Sounds wonderful! I will look into it. Thank you."

Learning to control our minds is incredible! When someone says something offensive to me, I can simply choose not to be offended. In fact, I can choose not to be angry, afraid, insecure, or anything else that I don't want to experience.

It's our thoughts about a situation, not the situation itself, that create our experience and memory of it. Or as Harold Pinter pointed out, "The past is what you remember, what you imagine you remember, convince yourself you remember, or pretend you remember."

— 4 —

BEHAVIOR PATTERNS

Take a piece of paper and fold it in half (not exactly in half, but close enough).

Now straighten it out and fold it again. The paper naturally folds at the crease that you've already created, right?

Our habits in life work in the exact same way: we mindlessly repeat the same pattern of behavior over and over again. So in order to change the way we habitually respond to the world, we have to make a new crease, so to speak.

Go ahead and fold that piece of paper in half again, but be precise this time (fold it exactly in the middle).

The more times you folded the piece of paper at the initial crease, the more difficult it will be to fold it at the new one.

If we apply enough deliberate intention, however, we can (and will) create a new pattern to follow. This requires mindful awareness of each and every thought we think, word we speak, and action we take. Of course it's easy to fall into old patterns when you first start out, but stay diligent because the new behavior will feel more natural after a short while; I promise!

Like a scar, the old crease will always be there. It will remind us of how we used to respond to certain situations, but it will no longer define who we are.

Mindfulness is exercised whenever we do one thing at a time. And despite the corporate glorification of being "busy," mindfulness is completely lost when we multi-task. If you're brushing your teeth while gathering the clothes that you're going to wear, then you're not mindfully brushing your teeth nor mindfully choosing an outfit. The same goes for when you prepare lunch and talk on the phone at the same time, eat dinner while watching TV, or make a to-do list in your head instead of trying to fall asleep. If you haven't trained your mind to stay focused on one thing at a time, then it will do whatever it wants to do, whenever it wants to do it, and you won't be able to "turn it off."

Mindfulness is a practice. It requires continuous attention until we can stay fully present and in complete control of our every thought, word, and action (as opposed to reaction). That's how we can end the cycle of continually doing what contributes to our unhappiness and follow our bliss instead.

The way society has been striving for happiness is an outdated behavior model that we seriously need to reevaluate. Whenever I'm invited to speak at various high schools across the United States, I draw a stick figure on one end of the blackboard and write the word "Happiness" on the other. I invite the kids to imagine that they are the stick figure on the left, and then I ask them what it would take to reach Happiness on the right. Every time they mention that something has to be accomplished before they'd be happy (like graduate, go to college, make lots of money, get married, buy a house, have kids, etc.), I draw a pothole on the path to happiness to represent what they would have to crawl out-of in order to get there.

As you can imagine, some holes are deeper and more difficult to crawl out of than others. If you can't be happy until you get your morning cup of a coffee, for example, then that's just a little bump in the road; no big deal. But if you think happiness isn't achievable until you have a certain amount of money in the bank or unless you slim down, then you're essentially paving a very difficult (sometimes impossible) road to happiness. This is especially true if you're doing this to impress other people, like your parents or friends.

We are essentially taking "Happiness," which is available to us right here and now, and pushing it far into the future. Instead of embracing happiness as our birthright, we've been treating it as a reward for certain accomplishments like graduation, a college degree, a six figure salary, and so on. The trick is to enjoy the journey itself!

I ask the students if they know anyone who already has a house, career, kids, and money, and whether those people are truly happy. They all start laughing because none of them has ever seen that recipe for happiness turn out, and yet they are all determined to try it for themselves. It's not just high-school kids who feel pressured to do this; adults everywhere are trying to find happiness by striving to complete a never-ending to-do list instead of simply choosing it regardless of what's going on.

Contrary to popular belief, happiness is not something that we have to pursue. It has nothing to do with what's happening around us, but everything to do with what's happening within.

Just as we felt sad or happy during the guided meditation that I mentioned earlier, we can actually choose how to internally navigate through every external situation in life. Again, I'm not suggesting that we bottle-up or ignore our ever-changing feelings, but it's important to remember the distinction between feelings and emotions. This distinction has helped me tremendously, and I hope it helps you too.

In order to relieve ourselves of emotional baggage we need to fire our internal storyteller, or, at the very least, stop taking the storyteller so seriously. The best way to do that is by being very mindful of how we complete any "I am" statements.

Instead of saying, "I am angry," try saying "I am feeling anger right now." This healthier alternative honors both the feeling and its fleeting nature without the risk of us identifying with something so temporary. Certain languages, like Spanish for example, have this distinction built-in: the verbs *ser* and *estar* both mean "to be," but *ser* refers to your permanent being (like where you're from), while *estar* is used to describe more temporary states (like anger, joy, sadness, or jealousy). Spanish students often use the following rhyme to remind themselves which of the two verbs to use: "For how you feel or where you are, always use the verb *estar*." But in English, simply adding the words "right now" at the end of many sentences is a great habit to get into.

Saying "I am angry" is extremely dangerous because it makes anger part of our identity, as does any word we place at the end of an "I am" sentence. When we say, "I am angry," we take a fleeting feeling and wear it like a jacket; we own it: "This is who I am!" And then we look at the world from the viewpoint of anger, which changes everything for the worse.

Anger, however, isn't a bad thing in-and-of-itself (no feeling is "good" nor "bad" since they all serve an important purpose). When we witness injustice, for example, our anger can propel us to act toward creating a positive change in the world, but we're better off doing it by promoting what we love instead of bashing what we hate.

I'm not against Monsanto, for example, I'm pro-organic food. (Calm down.. keep reading!) I'm also not angry at meat-eaters, I simply choose a plant-based diet. I'm not against men and women getting married, but I see no reason why two women or men shouldn't marry one another as well. I don't think large corporations are evil, I just try to support local businesses whenever I can. It's that simple. Instead of bashing what I hate, I promote what I love (it's better for my health).

We're not all activists in the rioting sense of the word, but we all vote with our wallets: we decide which companies get to stay in business and which do not. Grocery stores in Hawaii will continue selling mangoes that are imported from Ecuador (even though mangoes grow right there on the islands), as long as people in Hawaii keep buying the mangoes from Ecuador. There is nothing inherently "evil" about this... it just is what it is. We each have the personal responsibility to figure out which business practices to support and which to ignore. If you're against animal cruelty, for example, but have leather seats in your car, or use makeup that's been tested on animals, then you're not living in line with your values.

Some people say that anger is a good motivator to "do the right thing," but I believe compassion is even better. That's because anger can blind us when we're so busy protesting AGAINST something (thereby giving it more energy and attention) and then we're actually disturbing the peace (not just around us, but within). As Mother Teresa said, "If you invite me to an anti-war rally I won't go, but if you invite me to a pro-peace rally, I will be there!"

If anger fuels us, it can cause irreparable damage. When my parents got married, they made up a new last name because of an argument between my father's parents and my mother about who was going to pay for the wedding (or something trivial like that), and my mother wanted nothing to do with his family, let alone carry their name. In a moment of anger, both sides made some harsh remarks that my mother decided were unforgivable. A few years later, when my sister and I were born, we were never allowed to meet anyone from my father's side of the family.

My sister rebelled as a teenager and spent some time with one of our cousins on our father's side, and my mother's anger was immediately redirected toward a new traitor: my sister. And some 35 years later, when I went back to Israel to meet my father's brother and sister for the first time, as well as his dying mother and many of his distant cousins, my mother's anger was redirected once again, this time toward me.

That anger of hers is no longer a mere feeling, it's a full-blown emotion. It is a story about a feeling felt long ago, yet that story is just as true, valid, and real to my mother today as it was in the early 70's.

What neither parent realized was going to happen when they made up a new family name was that it communicated a simple and false lesson to a kid who didn't really understand what was going on; it taught me that it's perfectly okay to cut people out of your life if they do something you don't like (even if those people are related to you by blood).

At it turns out, I didn't understand the definition of the word "family" at all; I confused it with the word "relatives." Your "family" isn't necessarily blood related; it is the people in your life who want you in theirs; the people who accept you for who you are. They are the ones who would do anything to see you smile, and who love you no matter what. Blood makes you related, but it's loyalty that makes you family.

We've all heard the phrase "Blood is thicker than water," and I always assumed it meant that blood-related family is more important than anyone outside that circle. It wasn't until recently that I learned the origin of that phrase: "The blood of the covenant is thicker than the water of the womb." It literally means the opposite of what I always thought it did!

So how does a boy from Israel end up being named Timber Hawkeye? Well… everyone in my high school called me "Timber" because they couldn't correctly pronounce my Israeli birth name, and when my first graphic design was published in the mid-90's, the company that hired me to design their logo wanted to credit my full name for the design. I liked the nickname "Timber," and since there was no significance to the last name that my parents made up, I just blurted out the first cool name that came to mind, which was "Hawkeye," the name of the street on which I lived at the time. I thought the name had a nice ring to it, so I legally embraced it shortly thereafter, and I've been sporting it ever since.

What I had unintentionally done by changing my name was also let go of my parents' drama, and it felt great to be free of it. After all, emotional maturity means not being upset today by something that upset us yesterday.

We are the ones who reinforce the stories in our heads, so we are the only ones who can let those stories go. People often insist on clinging to their anger toward someone, for example, because, as they explain it, those people "deserve it." What they fail to realize is that their anger isn't affecting the people with whom they are angry, it is only harmful to themselves. Having witnessed what staying angry with someone for 30+ years has done to my mother, I've decided to never hold a grudge against anyone.

Like the old Buddhist saying goes: "Holding on to anger is like grasping a hot coal with the intention of throwing it at someone else; you are the one who gets burned."

Taking care of yourself is a declaration that you see your own worth and value. Not taking care of yourself conveys the exact opposite.

Emotional Maturity

means not being

upset today

by something that

upset you

yesterday.

— 5 —

GUILT TRIP

"I carried you in my womb for nine months; I gave birth to you!"

This was my mother's best argument, or at least the one she used most often, to explain why I must love and respect her as my mother (because she carried me in her womb and gave birth to me).

"The day I was born is the day your responsibility as my mother BEGAN," I wanted to say, "not the day it ended!" We clearly had very different definitions of what being a mother entailed, but I never dared say it out loud.

As far as I was concerned, the act of getting pregnant was the equivalent of applying for the job, and popping me out was like accepting the job. To truly be a mother, however, she would have actually had to mother (a verb, not a noun).

Now I realize that her parenting style was never the problem. She actually did what she thought was best (given her time, place, and circumstance). My parents met when they were 15 for crying out loud, and they got married at 18. The real problem was my long list of expectations of her; that's what caused my frustration and disappointment. I had this idea in my head of how a mother "should" be. It didn't matter how often she beat me if only she would come to my room at the end of the day for the ever-elusive "I'm sorry for overreacting" talk, but it never happened.

Like so many kids my age, I grew up watching *Who's the Boss?* I loved that no matter what Alyssa Milano did to upset her dad during certain episodes, they always had that apologetic talk at the end. I knew it was only a television show, but what else did I have to go on? Kids didn't talk to each other about what went on inside their houses. That's why I think it's important that we open up about it, even now. Otherwise, kids will continue to feel like they're the only ones going through whatever they're going through, and that's never the case.

If I had known how to clearly articulate and communicate my needs as a son, and if my mother could have truly listened, I think we would have avoided many years of aggravation and frustration with one another. It's sad that schools only teach us a language, but they do not teach us how to communicate.

As an adult, I had to forgive myself, forgive her, and then move on. Someone recently asked me how long it took me to forgive her, and to be honest, as soon as I stopped waiting for her to apologize, I was able to let it go.

Sometimes we wait for an apology from someone we feel has somehow "wronged" us. But since we now know that nobody can "make us feel" anything, and since we can forgive people without ever receiving an apology (they don't even have to be sorry), the act of forgiveness liberates us, not them; it's a gift you give yourself.

As you can see (and have surely experienced first hand), we have a lot more control over our emotional and mental states than we give ourselves credit for. As Carlos Castaneda succinctly articulated, "You can make yourself happy, or you can make yourself miserable; the amount of work is the same!"

Until you change your thinking, you will keep going in circles, recycling the same experiences over and over again.

What you allow

is what will

continue.

You teach people

how to treat you.

— 6 —

LEARNED BEHAVIOR

By the age of 10 I was already well versed in the Old Testament. I will never forget walking into a synagogue with my dad and stopping dead in my tracks as soon as the double doors opened. I "saw" a massive brain hovering in the middle of the room, with pipes coming out of it, plugged into everyone's head.

It was Yom Kippur (the day of atonement), and it felt so wrong to me that everyone used the same prayer to apologize to God for their past year's sins, while all I wanted to do was have a personal conversation with God. I wanted to express my deep appreciation for God's unconditional understanding and forgiveness, not to cry and beg for mercy (which felt as unnecessarily cruel as fasting for 24 hours did). I was only 10, but I told my dad that I never wanted to set foot inside a synagogue again. He told me that if I promise to go just one more time for my Bar Mitzvah when I turn 13, then he would never make me go again. Thank you, dad!

With driving prohibited on Yom Kippur (along with wearing leather shoes, taking a shower, and so on), I watched the procession of everyone walking to the synagogue, wearing the same facial expression, and it all felt very... staged.

Receiving instructions on how to properly emote (and what sort of behavior is expected of me) felt extremely unnatural; I wanted no part of it.

Since the day we were born, we've been watching everyone around us (from our parents to friends and even actors on television) emotionally react to any given situation (some more dramatically than others), so our own emotional reactivity is nothing more than learned behavior (monkey see; monkey do).

I'm not suggesting that we express our feelings any less (all of our feelings are completely valid, and it would actually be unnatural to feel nothing at all), but emotional reactivity is another thing altogether.

How we emote has a lot to do with what society deems appropriate or how we think others expect us to behave. We just play along because we either want their attention or fear their disappointment.

A few years ago, one of my dearest friends in Hawaii lost her husband when he stepped on a land-mine during the Gulf War. They were newlyweds in their early twenties, and she was saddened by his death, of course, but she wasn't devastated (certainly not to the degree expected of her at the televised military funeral).

She confessed to me that the big, dark, sunglasses she wore at the service were not to cover her tears but the lack thereof. Everyone expected her to wail and flail about, but much like me, she doesn't emote (which explains why we're such good friends, doesn't it?)

Her lack of emotions doesn't make her a robot or heartless; just rational, logical, grounded, and at peace. It is a sign of strength and emotional maturity, not of numbness. She was sad, but not reactive. I wonder why society judges that as a flaw?

Asking ourselves why we do things the way we've always done them is an interesting question to ponder, but it's also a trap. There are essentially two different therapeutic approaches to behavior modification: one method digs up the past to better understand the origin of our triggers by uncovering childhood experiences, old wounds, and buried memories; while the other method focuses on the present moment, right here and now, with the sole intention of determining what new thinking pattern is necessary to get us to where we want to go.

For example, if we have insecurities or believe that we're not worthy of love, we can either spend years in therapy to uncover the origin of that debilitating emotion (a story we have either told ourselves or heard from others over the course of many years); or we can acknowledge that the story is simply not true. Only then can we start to create a new thought process that works to our benefit (like making a new crease, if you would), to help us get to where we want to be right away (or as close to "right away" as possible).

In a nutshell, "Don't look back for TOO long because you're not going that way!"

The Buddha, once again, beautifully illustrated this point with a parable that I'm going to include in its entirety because it's as relate-able today as it was thousands of years ago:

> "A man is wounded with an arrow thickly smeared with poison. His friends and companions, kinsmen and relatives provide him with a surgeon, but the man says, 'I won't have this arrow removed until I know whether the man who wounded me was a noble warrior, a priest, a merchant, or a worker.'
>
> He would say, 'I won't have this arrow removed until I know the given name and clan name of the man who wounded me... until I know whether he was tall, medium, or short... until I know whether he was dark or golden-colored... until I know his home village, town, or city... until I know whether the bow with which I was wounded was a long bow or a crossbow... until I know whether the bowstring with which I was wounded was fiber, bamboo, hemp, or bark... until I know whether the shaft with which I was wounded was wild or cultivated... until I know whether the feathers of the shaft with which I was wounded were those of a vulture, a stork, a hawk, a peacock, or another bird... until I know whether the shaft with which I was wounded was bound with the sinew of an ox, a water buffalo, or a monkey.'

He would say, 'I won't have this arrow removed until I know whether the shaft with which I was wounded was that of a common arrow, a curved arrow, a barbed, calf-toothed, or an oleander arrow.'

But the man would sooner die, and those things would still remain unknown to him."

I say get that arrow out of there right away, and enjoy your life immediately! Who, what, where, when, or why you were shot is completely irrelevant. You can spend your entire life trying to make sense of things that don't make sense.

As Alan Moore summarized, "The past cannot hurt you anymore... Not unless you let it!"

You can't love
yourself if you
still hate or
resent the experiences
that shaped you
(Yes, all of them).

— 7 —

COHESION

It's very embarrassing to admit, but prior to moving to the United States, before my first year of high school, I was extremely ignorant of how the world's population was divided. I seriously thought all Africans lived in Africa, Asians in Asia, Indians in India, and so on. It never occurred to me that America would be home to such a diversity of races and religions, and my family moved to one of the most culturally rich cities in one of the most racially diverse states: San Francisco, California. I was immediately fascinated, intrigued, and curious. I transitioned from a town populated by only two thousand people to a city of almost a million! The high school I attended had 3,000 students, and Caucasians like me were a small minority. It was incredible!

When I first started school, the administration placed me in ESL classes (English as a Second Language). The only English words I knew at the time were "Yes, no, hi, and bye," but it was all the vocabulary I needed to start a conversation with all the exotic people who caught my eye: a gorgeous girl named Judy from Burma, a striking guy from the Philippines named Seth, the stern Mr. Kawakami from Japan, and the whimsical

Ms. Vargas from Mexico. It was a cultural melting pot, and I wanted to know everything about everyone!

As soon as my English improved and I was placed in the same classes as everyone else, nothing stopped me from striking up a conversation with Kheesha (the class clown from Chicago), or Jacob (the tall jock from Ohio). Everyone intrigued me and piqued my curiosity. And even though I was bullied and constantly made fun-of for being so strange and awkward, I wasn't deterred.

Moving from one country to another as a teenager has probably benefited me in more ways than I can imagine. In contrast to many immigrants who do everything they can to cling to their culture and language, I just wanted to be the All American Kid.

Television depicted what an American teenager's life was like, and I did everything I could to emulate each and every aspect of that image: from newspaper delivery on my bike around the neighborhood, to wearing a bandana just like the one that Axl Rose was wearing in the poster that hung above my bed next to a picture of Alyssa Milano. I was a very confused teenager; can you tell?

Whenever someone pointed out that I was saying an English word with an Israeli accent, I made a mental note to never say it that way again. "Peelow" became "pillow," eating falafel was traded for Whoppers at Burger King, and hummus swapped places with ranch dressing. Admittedly, not all the changes were upgrades.

As an outsider, there were many things that I didn't initially understand, and perhaps never would, but putting forth the intention and effort to understand them went a very long way.

It is impossible for anyone to experience the world from another's perspective. Even walking a mile in their shoes wouldn't be the same because we each bring our own perspective to the path.

If we take the time to listen to people's stories, however, with the intention of understanding them (not to criticize or condemn them), a magical thing occurs: judgment gives way to compassion.

The novelty of diversity in high school wore off a bit when my being openly Jewish and Israeli resulted in swastikas carved on my hallway locker, which I promptly covered with bumper stickers. It was the early nineties, so I think this was done by guys who were jealous of me dating the gorgeous Russian exchange student, not because I was Jewish, but we'll never know. All I know is that I hated high school after the locker incident, and I only made new friends in one of two ways: through my cousins (who all went to a different school than me), or through an after-school program I attended to become a Holocaust docent so I could turn around and teach kids about World War II.

As a Holocaust docent, I studied with survivors so I could share their stories with the next generation. Most students reacted to learning about the heartbreaking events with confusion as to how any human can abuse another to that extent. It became clear to me that to understand the full story, we must try to understand the aggressors and what drives people to commit such atrocities.

Nazi Germany may have been a thing of the past, but the Ku Klux Klan was still frequently seen on TV when I was in high school (more on Jerry Springer than in the news, but still).

Hearing a Klan member speak of his childhood, I learned about a boy who was regularly beaten and abused in a broken home. He was raised in a hostile and violent environment during a time, place, and circumstance where racism was rampant. He was also ridiculed at school and on the playground, when all he wanted was to fit in, the same way we all did in our youth.

With very little will to live, this young boy was on the verge of suicide. He was almost broken by his environment when he met the "brotherhood," which offered him unity, protection, and, most importantly, a place to call home.

These groups, regardless of the form they take, almost always share a common enemy figure, for it assures cohesion among its members (it gives everyone something to fight against, which is one of the strongest uniting forces in a community).

Just look at sports these days: people can't simply root for the Seattle Seahawks without hating the Green Bay Packers. And in the U.K., fans of opposing soccer teams are terribly hostile toward each other one week, but they immediately band together as one when England plays France. Like the old proverb suggests, "The enemy of my enemy is my friend" (a terrible common denominator for unity with devastating results, if you ask me).

The young boy who grew up to be a member of the KKK was grateful for the Klan's support when his own family mistreated him, so he pledged allegiance to the brotherhood, and he was willing to do just about anything to ensure his continued acceptance in their circle.

Conditional love, in his eyes, was better than no love at all. And we've all settled for it at one point or another. Some of us still do.

Our intention to connect with others through understanding can open our hearts and minds, taking us away from judgment, disdain, and hatred, toward empathy and compassion instead.

I'm not suggesting we join their group or condone their behavior, nor am I saying that understanding a terrorist, a rapist, or a murderer, justifies what they do. But when we try to understand them, we do away with any hatred or animosity that we harbor (which is destructive and often the same driving force behind the very actions we condemn), and replace it with compassion (which is healing, patient, kind, and potentially forgiving).

As Thich Nhat Hanh so concisely put it, "When a person is causing harm to others, it is because he or she is suffering deeply within themselves, and that pain spills over. They do not need punishment; what they need is our help; that is the message they are sending."

I admit that I've done some terrible things in my life, and I include judging other people among them. Jesus was onto something when he said, "Let the one who has never sinned throw the first stone," and the crowd stood silent.

If I've been able to change from the person I was into who I am today, then everyone deserves the same opportunity to grow. If you want to eliminate any chance of ever thinking less of someone else, I suggest living by Walt Whitman's invitation to always "Be curious, not judgmental."

— 8 —

PARENT FIGURES

As soon as I graduated high school, just as I was about to move away for college, my girlfriend of two years told me she was pregnant. We had always used protection, and she was taking birth control pills, so I initially wondered if she was only telling me this to delay the inevitable breakup when I leave town (could I have been more arrogant?).

Alisha was epileptic, and it turned out the medicine she was taking for epilepsy at the time canceled out the birth control pills. Condoms don't always work, and we both learned the important lesson (albeit too late), that if you're not ready to face the consequences, you're not ready to do the deed.

Though Alisha was against abortion at the time, we realized how unrealistic it is for anyone to make decisions about hypothetical situations ahead of time. It's impossible for us to know how we would react if/when we find ourselves having to actually make them.

If Alisha went off the medication to continue the pregnancy, she would have been prone to violent and potentially lethal seizures. And if she kept taking the medication while pregnant, not only would birth defects be almost certain, but doing so would also put her and the baby's life in danger.

This difficult decision was nobody's to make but Alisha's. My commitment was to support her and hold her hand, be it in the delivery room or at the clinic.

What made a hard decision even more difficult were the protesters outside the clinic who were completely insensitive to the fact that this procedure wasn't Alisha's first choice; she technically had no choice. Try telling that to the men and women who called her a murderer as we walked into the clinic with tears in our eyes... as if that day wasn't hard enough already. Always remember that everyone is fighting an internal battle that you know absolutely nothing about.

Alisha's mother was the only adult we told about the pregnancy because my parents would have been extremely angry, not so much because I got a girl pregnant, but because Alisha was Catholic.

When we moved from Israel to San Francisco, my parents told me that if I so much as consider dating a girl who isn't Jewish, they would send me back to Israel to serve in the military (something they knew I didn't want to do).

It was a cruel joke to send their teenage boy to a public school in one of the most culturally diverse cities yet limit his dating options to Jewish girls alone. It was like taking your kid to an ice cream shop but only allowing him to order vanilla when there are over thirty flavors from which to choose.

Alisha wasn't the first girl I dated who wasn't Jewish. I remember trying to reason with my parents to let me date Kelly, a Methodist, by telling them how nice, smart, and pretty she was, but none of that mattered to them. They forbade me from seeing her again, but I simply waited a couple of weeks and then told them I had met a new girl named Rebecca (and said this one was Jewish). They didn't know Rebecca didn't exist and that I was talking about Kelly because they had never met her, and we ended up seeing each other for a few months.

My room was adjacent to my parents' bedroom, and if I looked through the heating vent on my side, I could see directly into their room at floor level. One day, while talking to my girlfriend on the phone, I got down on my knees to look through the heating vent, and there were my mother's feet, sitting still at the edge of the bed, just listening to my phone conversation. I essentially learned to lie to my parents because telling them the truth wasn't an option; I couldn't trust them to love or accept me unconditionally.

Whenever I disobeyed my parents' demands, shoes were my mother's weapon-of-choice (household slippers with a firm rubber sole were her favorite, she said, because they made a very rewarding "pop" sound with every swing). I vividly recall curling up in the fetal position on the floor of my room with Mother hovering over me in one of her fits of rage, swinging her shoe against my skin over and over again, when all of a sudden there was a knock on the front door (neighbors frequently came over unannounced in those days). Mother dropped the shoe, straightened her hair and posture, told me to stay quiet in my room, and answered the door in the most polite, pleasant voice one would expect. Her ability to "save face" frightened me more than any blow.

I witnessed it again a couple of years later when she banged her toe against the dresser, dropped to the floor, and grabbed her foot in what appeared to be excruciating pain. Rocking back-and-forth, she was crying, practically wailing, when the phone on the bedside table rang. She immediately got up, picked up the receiver, and said, "Hello?" as if nothing had happened.

The vision I have of my mother is of a faceless woman in a small room with four walls, each covered with hundreds of masks. And before she steps out of that room, she picks a mask off the wall, puts it on, and plays the part. To this day, I don't think anyone has ever seen her true face. Like the actor, Gabriel Byrne, who played a priest in *Stigmata* yet portrayed the devil in *End of Days*, my mother could convince you of her character in one moment, then play its opposite in another.

At the end of the day, our parents either teach us how to be or how not to be, but they are teachers either way.

The visual of that room with masks on the wall has stuck with me over the years. It served as a constant reminder to always be truthful, transparent, and show the real me no matter what (perhaps to a fault). I have never altered the way I speak or carry myself, whether in the company of friends, bosses, strangers, or clergy. I always choose to be honest instead of polite, opting for truth over manners. Most importantly, I simply refuse to lie, be it by omission or otherwise.

It's because I think honesty is best that I find it's better to have a direct relationship with God instead of having it through religion; God loves us unconditionally, after all, without any expectations, while religion has a set of standards for us to meet (with some churches appending those standards even more). Perhaps it's because religion is man-made and therefore modeled after human behavior, whereas God's love has no prerequisites or boundaries. We can be who we are and God would still love and accept us no matter what, but we sadly have to change who we are if we want religion to see us as worthy of God's love.

Religion depicts God as a parent figure with us as children trying to win God's affection in the same way we try to win our parents' love (by doing what we are told). I don't need to change for God to love me, and I refuse to change to appease others. In the words of the beautiful Kurt Cobain, "I would rather be hated for who I am than loved for who I am not."

Anyone who grows
mentally, skillfully, or
spiritually, knows that
growth is not
found in comfort.

— 9 —

TRANSPARENCY

I was raised in a household with parents who explicitly instructed my sister and I to never, under any circumstances, discuss with others what went on inside our house (let alone publish a book about it). It never occurred to me that it was because some of what was going on was inappropriate or downright illegal. I just thought every family kept its secrets hidden and that's just the way the world worked.

The intention behind airing our dirty laundry is not to spite my parents. I used to feel shame about my struggles because nobody else spoke of their issues so I thought I was the only one. Now I know that repression leads to depression and that pain does not decompose when you bury it. When I started talking with others about my upbringing, I realized there was never a reason to feel lonely; we're all battling very similar demons. What I genuinely hope is that revealing my darkness and giving it a voice would heal our silenced wounds and propel us forward in continuous search for transparency in all things.

Loneliness is not a feeling like sadness or sorrow; it's an emotional craving more closely related to addiction than to a genuine feeling like hurt or jealousy.

There is a big difference between being alone and being lonely. "Alone" simply means in solitude (a party of one). It does not imply loneliness, nor is loneliness a by-product of being alone.

When I was young and didn't tell anyone about my internal struggles, I felt incredibly lonely even though I was surrounded by friends. As Paul Tournier said, "Nothing makes us more lonely than our secrets."

If we pretend to be someone we are not in order to be accepted by others, keep our true identity secret, or choose to never share our true thoughts and feelings with the people who are closest to us, then loneliness will set in like a dark cloud that completely obliterates the brightness of the sun (whether we're alone or in a room full of people).

The secret is to approve of our own decisions in life instead of looking to others for acceptance or validation. And when we're at peace with who we are, then we can be open and vulnerable with everyone in our lives without fear. People will actually relate to what we're going through, not judge us for our insecurities. You see, vulnerability is our greatest strength, not weakness. It unites us and connects us to one another, and then we never feel lonely (even when we're alone). As Wayne Dyer put it, "You cannot be lonely if you like the person you're alone with."

— 10 —

CONSUMPTION

My friend Lauren introduced me to Eknath Easwaran, from whom I've adopted many of the mindfulness tools that I still utilize today. Through his books and public talks, he invites us to consider that we not only eat with our mouths, we consume with our eyes and our ears as well. We are constantly taking in information (visually and audibly) and, as the old saying goes, we are what we eat. At some point in the late nineties, I realized that a lot of the shows and movies I was watching, as well as the music I was listening to, were violent, negative, angry, and drama-laden. I needed to go on a serious media-diet!

I quit watching CNN (Constantly Negative News), stopped reading newspapers (which no longer had any sense of objectivity), and began minimizing my exposure to advertisements through magazines or other forms of media as much as possible. I basically stopped consuming all the gossip, drama, negativity, paranoia, and fear that surrounds us. If I hadn't, I would have inevitably become negative myself, paranoid, and fearful (like so many others).

Instead, I choose to read books, watch documentaries, meditate, go for long walks or hikes, and take it upon myself to look for the beauty in the world because they aren't showing it on TV. Essentially, I stopped watching other people's lives on television and started living my own.

At first, the only difference I noticed was that I didn't have anything to talk to people about around the water cooler at the office (not knowing what happened on *Ally McBeal* the night before had its consequences). But after a few years of non-exposure, I realized that something greater had changed: all of my thoughts were now my own. I wasn't being told, subliminally or otherwise, what to eat or listen to, what to buy or what's hip, new or modern. I felt no pressure to own anything that I didn't even know existed, nor was I fearful of leaving my house because of crime on the streets. Instead of craving what the digitally-enhanced pictures of food tried to pitch as the latest hunger quencher, my body told me what it was hungry for, and strangely enough, it was never hungry for anything fried... imagine that!

I recently sat down to watch a few episodes of a mainstream sitcom, and I was shocked by what kind of language and behavior between friends, siblings, parents and their children, and even toward strangers, was depicted as "perfectly normal." The characters were rude, dismissive, accusatory, lying, backstabbing, cheating, dramatic, and emotionally unstable, all of which was being presented to us as a form of entertainment (and still is). And with society emulating what they see on television (especially in some shows considered "Reality TV,") it's no wonder kids today (and a fair share of adults), treat each other with such hostility. We can't live a positive life with a negative attitude; it's just not possible.

Newscasters and reporters bend over backwards to pitch a story. No longer is it sufficient to cover the latest conflict with North Korea, for example, but it's somehow necessary to tell us what Jennifer Lopez thinks about it, and, to be perfectly honest, I'm not interested; no offense to J-Lo.

So, yes, I rely on my friends to tell me about the really important stuff that goes on in the world, but it's amazing how rarely they deem anything important enough to share with me. In fact, whenever I tell people that I don't watch TV, most of them respond by saying, "You're not missing anything!"

So when it comes to the news, as Mark Twain pointed out, "If you don't read the newspaper, then you are uninformed. But if you do read the newspaper, then you are misinformed."

You will stop

attracting certain people

into your life

when you heal the part

of you that once

needed them.

Let them go.

— 11 —

EPIPHANY

With limited exposure to media, I have reduced the amount of negativity in my life, and it feels great. But that's only half the equation. What about my own contribution to the world? Are my thoughts, words, and actions part of the problem? And if so, how can I make them part of the solution?

There is an ancient Arab proverb about mindful speech that invites us to imagine three gatekeepers in our throat whose jobs are to ensure that certain words don't go past our lips (sort of like airport security, except you get to keep your shoes on).

It's very simple: whenever you're about to say something, the first gatekeeper asks, "Is what you're about to say true?" And if it's true, then the words proceed to the next gate, where the second guard asks, "Is what you're about to say necessary?" (This is where I personally add the question Is it necessary to be said by ME? because some things are true and need to be said, but it's rarely my place to say them, you know?) If what you're about to say is indeed true and necessary, then the words proceed to the third and final gatekeeper who asks, "Is what you're about to say kind?"

Only if what you have to say is true, necessary, AND kind, do you actually say it, email, post, text, or tweet it. And if you can't be kind, be quiet!

This practice of mindful speech raised my awareness in every aspect of life, especially concerning my social circle.

After a decade of living in and around Northern California's Bay Area, I finally decided it was time to leave. For as long as I could remember, I would call Steve (the "leader of the pack") every Friday night to find out which club we were hitting that weekend. It was usually a randomly selected nightclub anywhere between Palo Alto and Sacramento. We would all get together, party, have fun, and promise to do it all again the following weekend.

We saw each other regularly, but there was always loud music, dancing, and a whole lot of alcohol involved. So even though I would see Brian, Connie, Kerri, Garret, Jordan, and countless others, I had no idea how any of them were actually holding up in life, with what they were currently struggling, or what kept them up at night. And before I knew it, months would go by without me having any good, quiet, quality one-on-one conversations with any of them.

Be it a rough week at work, a birthday celebration, new crushes or broken relationships, we basically found any excuse to drink and party, but we made no time to actually talk to one another.

I longed for a deeper connection with people and to be less concerned with how many friends surrounded me, and more focused on how well I knew the few who truly cared. This was long before texting and social media was around, when you actually had to call someone to talk to them.

As a social experiment to determine who was a friend and who was merely an acquaintance, I decided to see how long it would take for any of them to call me if I simply stopped showing up on the weekends. Sadly, not a single one of them ever called. It turns out that I had over 100 acquaintances but not a single friend to call my own (friends make time, acquaintances make excuses; that's how you know).

For a fresh start, I packed my things and moved to Seattle, where I didn't know anybody. Socially, I had the choice to either meet new people and tag along with whatever they liked to do (which would essentially repeat the old cycle from the Bay), or I could take some time to discover who I was, what my own hobbies were, and what I actually enjoyed doing for the first time in my life.

Hiking was at the top of my list (I've always loved the outdoors, and Seattle offers amazing trails through the Cascades and Olympic Mountains). So yes, I went hiking alone, but it wasn't long before I met other people on the trails who obviously also like to hike! This proved to also be true with kayaking, yoga, and rollerblading. But it was the volleyball circuit that introduced me to my largest social circle, which I would have never even discovered had I not been brave enough to dive into it alone. We regularly played at a local gym in the winter, or we set up multiple nets at Green Lake, Golden Gardens, and Alki Beach when the sun was out.

Between indoor, beach, and grass volleyball, tennis, hiking, and rock climbing, the same guy who failed physical education in high school was suddenly turning into quite the athlete, and this completely changed my life!

Career-wise in Seattle, I was earning less than half of what I made in San Francisco, but it didn't matter; I was happier in the Pacific Northwest than I had ever been anywhere else. And that's when I realized that my happiness had nothing to do with my income.

This epiphany snowballed into an entirely new lifestyle fueled by passion instead of greed. Less became more, and my job did not define me in any way whatsoever; it was just something I did between 8 and 5. Since the sun in Seattle doesn't set until 10 o'clock at night in the summertime, my day was just starting when I left work at 5pm, not ending.

If someone could have a mid-life crisis in their twenties, I was definitely having mine! To align my lifestyle with what I was learning from Eknath Easwaran about treating our bodies the way we would treat the only jacket we get to wear in our lifetime, I started taking really good care of myself by eating right, abstaining from alcohol and tobacco, and spending a lot of time outdoors. The results were incredible. The move to Seattle turned out to be the birth of a new me.

Sadly, the cost of my prior life in San Francisco accrued interest. Literally. The total amount of debt I had charged on my credit cards in California officially exceeded my new annual income in Washington. Determined to pay it off, I simply stuck to doing more of what I enjoyed (like all of that wonderful time outdoors that didn't cost a thing), and I was debt-free in less than five years; the greatest feeling in the world!

Paying off my debt required some serious self-control, determination, and grit (qualities that have proven to be extremely beneficial in every aspect of my life thereafter, so I'm glad I started exercising them when I did).

Every time I was tempted to buy a cup of coffee or eat at a restaurant instead of at home, it felt like I was digging myself a deeper hole instead of trying to climb out of one. A Swedish proverb that helped me remember my goal was, "He who buys what he does not need steals from himself."

I don't mourn the loss of my acquaintances in San Francisco because they were replaced with true friends in Seattle, and I don't miss eating meat or drinking alcohol because that was replaced with feeling healthy all the time. You see, none of it was a sacrifice, it was all an exchange; an upgrade. And in the same token, letting go of dogma, tradition, ritual, and religion to directly embrace faith instead, felt like a huge improvement.

As Lenny Bruce noticed, "Every day people are straying away from the church and going back to God." It's a beautiful thing to see!

Your life became a
struggle when you
turned your
preferences into
needs.

— 12 —

PERSPECTIVE

When the Twin Towers fell in New York City, I was on the bus in Seattle on my way to work. Knowing that I don't watch television or listen to the radio, a friend rightfully figured that I wouldn't know what was going on, so he called me with the news. When my cell phone rang, he was on the other end screaming, "World War III just started!"

Seminars in Non-Violent Communication (NVC) teach us, among other things, to distinguish between a judgment and an observation. Simply put, an observation is what can essentially be videotaped without audio, and a judgment is, quite often, the narrative.

Observation: buildings were blown up in Manhattan.

Judgment: the third World War is upon us.

Think of them as "fact versus truth," as we explored earlier. Fact: this just happened. Truth: this is what it means to me, and anyone who chooses to believe anything different is wrong (truths are starting to sound as flaky as feelings, aren't they?)

Everything we experience is all about perspective. You and your friend can look at a work of art, for example, and if you tell them what you see before they form their own opinion, chances are they'll see the same thing you do. But if you show it to them without any commentary, they will assign their own meaning to it. Conflict arises when we want other people to validate our interpretation of the world by seeing it the same way we do.

With that mentality, it's easy to understand why wars start in the first place, right? The wars outside of us simply reflect the turmoil within. It's therefore inner peace that will lead to world peace, not the other way around.

Those who routinely internalize their conflicts are the ones who later participate in acts of terror themselves. That's what emotions do: they cloud our better judgment. This is why it's absurd to kill someone in order to prove that killing is wrong, yet people and governments do it all the time.

This either sounds completely rational to you or utterly insensitive, depending on how emotionally reactive you normally are. But either way, I hope you see the logic behind this line of thinking. Logic, after all, plays a very important role in my journey to having faith, which sounds crazy (I know), because faith is illogical.

To better illustrate this distinction between judgment and observation, let's say I'm in San Francisco and I want to drive to Los Angeles (which is to the south). If I'm heading north when I pull off the freeway to ask you for directions and you tell me that I'm going the wrong way, you wouldn't be making a judgment, you'd be making an observation. That's because you, personally, have no preference as to where I go; you're merely pointing out that if my intention is to get to Los Angeles from San Francisco, then I need to head south, not north. So by saying, "You're going the wrong way," you're making an observation, not a judgment. I hope that makes sense.

However, if I pull off the freeway to ask you for directions, and you tell me I'm crazy for wanting to go to Los Angeles because it's smoggy and terrible, then you'd be making a judgment, not an observation (and you'd be dishing out some unsolicited advice in the process).

When I call my friends with a dilemma, they first ask me what I'm hoping to achieve through my proposed actions. This helps them mirror back to me whether the decision I'm about to make will get me closer to, or further from, the results I'm hoping to get (just like giving directions). And when my friends call me with a problem, I offer myself as a mirror in return.

Laura called me distressed one day saying, "I'm financially strapped because my husband and I are trying to have another child!"

While she doesn't see the answer in the question because she's too close to the problem, it's easy for an outsider to reflect that perhaps trying to have a second kid while already financially strapped is not such a great idea.

By having no personal attachment to the outcome, we can make a truly unbiased observation of any situation (even our own). Haven't you noticed how we're better at giving someone else the same advice that we need to follow ourselves? It's because we're not emotionally invested in someone else's decision like we are with our own. Again, emotions are potholes on an otherwise smooth path toward euphoria. The trick is to focus on the journey, not the destination, so we can have no emotional attachment to the outcome.

Having faith, as I said earlier, is embracing the unknown; taking a step forward when you're not sure where it will lead (not because you're a daredevil, but because scary as that step might be, it's not nearly as scary as staying stuck). We more frequently regret steps that we haven't taken in life than the steps we have. Besides, how can we grow if we don't have faith that all of our past experiences were not mistakes but rather necessary steps to equip us with the strength needed to make it through what's ahead?

Another friend recently broke down and said to me, "I've never been happy. It simply doesn't exist for me or within me."

To which I gave the following response:

> "At this point, Pat, it's a self-fulfilling prophecy. You've been saying this for so long that it has become part of your identity. You truly believe that happiness doesn't exist for you, which is why you can't see it even though it's within your reach (we

can't see what we don't believe exists). First things first: look at the words with which you describe your day, your life, and the world around you. If they're all negative, then there's your answer. Happiness is not about seeing the glass as half full instead of half empty, it's about being grateful to have a glass in the first place. Gratitude is the key to happiness, not the other way around. It doesn't matter how much more "stuff" you buy in an attempt to make yourself happy if you can't even be happy with what you already have.

Mindfulness is about retraining the mind to create new thought and behavior patterns because your old patterns clearly don't work, Pat. Since being miserable is such a core part of your identity, you have to be extremely willing to let go of whatever you thought was true until now and start fresh.

This has nothing to do with anyone else in your life (expecting someone else to make you happy is the surest way to be sad). Happiness is an inside job, and you have to be willing to do the work. If you're addicted to your misery, you might just need some rehab-type restructuring, but you have to want to be happy more than you want to keep doing everything the same way you have been so far. There's no secret here, as Will Rogers said, 'If you find yourself in a hole, the first thing to do is stop digging!'"

I was afraid that I may have been too direct with her, but she said it was exactly what she needed to hear. This conversation worked because she was open to hearing that reflection. Try giving it to someone who didn't ask for it (or isn't ready for it), and you'd lose a friend and possibly make matters worse.

Unfortunately, many people only claim to want a way out of their suffering but they aren't actually willing to do the work necessary to get there. Luckily, Pat was ready and willing to let go of anything and everything that was detrimental to her happiness (job, relationship, habitual tendencies, the language she used to identify herself, etc.), and she turned her life around.

As a mirror, so to speak, it's important not to get attached to an end result in other people's lives. We can give people all the advice, information, data, and facts they need to make a rational decision, but we can't force them to make it. In other words, you can lead them to knowledge but you can't make them think. You cannot want something for someone more than they want it for themselves.

Many people are proud of being brutally honest and always saying what's on their mind with no sugar coating. I should know... I used to be that guy. I didn't care if my honesty hurt people because, in my mind, I was telling them the truth and, at the end of the day, the truth heals, right? Well, I still believe it's important to always be honest, but honesty is best served with a side order of tact. As Isaac Newton beautifully said, "Tact is the art of making a point without making an enemy."

The beauty of committing to a life of radical honesty (not brutal honesty), non-violent communication, and the practice of the three gate keepers (only saying what is true, necessary, and kind), is that the friends we make on this journey are more likely to stick with us through it all, not only when we say or do something that they "like."

The first of the *Four Agreements* by don Miguel Ruiz is to be impeccable with our words, which goes beyond being honest, to acknowledging that words have the power to create or to destroy. He invites us to "speak with integrity, to say only what we mean, avoid using language to speak against ourselves or to gossip about others, and, instead, to use the power of our words in the direction of truth and love."

If the method of the three gatekeepers doesn't work for you in filtering out the detrimental, then a quote from Gandhi to remember when considering mindful speech is to simply "not speak unless it improves the silence."

You can't calm the storm,

so stop trying. What you

CAN do is calm yourself...

the storm will pass.

— 13 —

INSTRUMENT OF PEACE

Thanks to an invitation by Eknath Easwaran in his book *Passage Meditation*, I've been meditating with the prayer of Saint Francis of Assisi for many years. I first read the book in 1993, then again ten years later, and I was shocked to rediscover some amazing insight that I apparently wasn't ready to absorb when I first read it ten years prior. This is why I often re-read inspirational books every few years. I seem to find something new to appreciate every time, not because the text in the book has changed, but because I have.

Although the prayer is beautiful, practical, psychologically and spiritually sound with great intentions, I initially had difficulty reciting it each morning because I found it very discouraging (I'll explain why in a minute).

The prayer is addressed to "God," "Lord," or "Divine Master," but that doesn't bother me because I take those terms rather lightly these days. I see them as a reference to a higher power within each of us, not outside of us, and that power is capable of creating, loving, giving, and forgiving.

Before I explain how I slightly modified the prayer from its original form (I don't think Saint Francis would mind), I am going to share it with you the way it was first written. See if you can guess what portion of the prayer felt counterproductive to me, and why I had to change it:

> "Lord, make me an instrument of thy peace.
> Where there is hatred, let me sow love;
> where there is injury, pardon;
> where there is doubt, faith;
> where there is despair, hope;
> where there is darkness, light;
> where there is sadness, joy.
>
> O' Divine Master,
> grant that I shall not so much seek to be consoled
> as to console,
> to be understood as to understand,
> or to be loved as to love.
> For it's in giving that we receive;
> it's in pardoning that we are pardoned;
> and it's in dying to self that we are born to eternal life."

The portion with which I struggled was, "Make me an instrument of thy peace," because it implied that I wasn't already. I found it detrimental to start my day from a place of lack, so I changed it a little bit. I now say, "I AM an instrument of peace," and then go on from there.

It is very empowering, and it beautifully sets the tone and intention for the rest of the day. Here is my version:

"Lord, I AM an instrument of peace.
Where there is hatred, I shall sow love;
where there is injury, pardon;
where there is doubt, faith;
where there is despair, hope;
where there is darkness, light;
where there is sadness, joy.

O' Divine Master,
I shall not so much seek to be consoled as to console;
to be understood as to understand;
or to be loved as to love.
For it's in giving that we receive;
it's in pardoning that we are pardoned;
and it's in dying to self that we are born to eternal life"

The last line, as I understand it, means that when we no longer identify with our "self" (with the ego), as somehow separate from others, then we see our place in the grandest scheme of things and realize that we never truly die but rather change form. I don't mean we return as a snail, but we continue to live through the lasting impact we've made on the lives of others. I don't give much thought to life after death; to be honest, I try to stay focused on life before death.

It is somewhat embarrassing to admit, but I completely misunderstood the Prayer of Saint Francis during the first few years that I meditated with it every morning. I thought it was a calling for us to go out in the world as instruments of peace and wherever we see hatred, to sow love. Where there is injury, pardon; where there is doubt, faith; where there is despair, hope; where there is darkness, light; and where there is sadness, joy. But how could I possibly spread love into the world when I, myself, still had hatred within me? We cannot give what we do not have; it's just not possible.

Only after making one more alteration to the prayer did it finally become clear that what I had to do was work on myself instead of trying to fix others. "Where there is hatred WITHIN, I shall sow love," etc.

The prayer empowered me to accept Gandhi's invitation to be the change I wanted to see in the world. At first I thought it was slightly selfish to focus on myself, but when my intention is to use this personal development to be of better service to others, it's as selfless as can be.

Our job isn't to go around trying to save people, or to drag them kicking and screaming, hoping that in the end they will thank us. In fact, I hope we continue to give to others without expecting anything in return (not even a thank you), because that is unconditional kindness; everything else is ego.

All we can do is live a healthy life and trust that those with eyes to see will pay attention. Our actions will always speak louder than our words, so my life is my message.

"But what if I witness someone doing something wrong?" I am often asked. "Shouldn't I say anything?"

We can't fight discrimination with discrimination. In fact, we don't need to fight at all; just love. Do you think your anger and frustration are going to stop other people's anger and frustration, or will it only fan their flames?

Here's a great example of why it's a good practice to be kind or be quiet:

I saw a woman yelling at a guy for throwing his soda bottle in the trashcan instead of the recycling bin, which was conveniently placed right beside it. "What are you doing?!?!" She screamed at him, "Aren't you concerned about the environment?"

He just looked at her and said, "Lady, I just downed a bacon double cheeseburger with a Pepsi, and I'm about to smoke another cigarette. I'm obviously not concerned about my own health, so what makes you think I give a %^&* about the environment?"

We can all learn a very important lesson from her outburst and from his honest reply: know your audience!

If changing the world is your fight, it will leave you exhausted. But if changing the world is simply your way of being, then it will be effortless. Or, as Rumi poetically exclaimed, "Yesterday I was clever so I wanted to change the world; today I am wise, so I am changing myself."

We are not all in a
position to help others in
some big, life-changing
way, but we are all
in a position not to
harm them.

— 14 —

PARADISE

Before we can accept Gandhi's invitation to be the change we wish to see in the world, let's take a step back to better assess what changes we actually want. Clearly, there is too much fear, violence, pride, and greed in the world, all of which cause conflict and wars (both within and around us), so logic dictates that greed, hatred, and ignorance would have to be the first things to eliminate, right? At least that's what is chanted every morning at Zen monasteries around the world: "Greed, Hatred, and Ignorance rise endlessly, I vow to abandon them."

Not so easy!

Not only was I not being an instrument of peace, as Saint Francis invites us to be, I was operating under the same blind mentality that contributes to the vicious cycle of problems that everyone else was complaining about: I was making choices that I thought I "had to make" without realizing that I could actually un-choose them at any moment. What I truly wanted (and what I gather everyone in the world is looking for), is an uncomplicated, simple life (no headaches, no stress, no anxiety... just peaceful serenity, and blissful calm). So why was I making one decision after another that added complications to my life and steered me further and further away from the simplicity I truly wanted? I wasn't just running on a hamster wheel, I built the darn thing!

Successfully stopping all of my exposure to media was a great first step, as was paying off my debt, but I was still operating on old programming. "Of course I have to work full time," I used to think. "How else would I be able to afford the condo, the car, and the cell phone? I NEED that full time job…" or so I thought.

Tyler Durden said, "The things you own end up owning you. And it's not until you lose everything that you are free to do anything!" That quote can be applied not just to losing material possessions, but letting go of our fears, insecurities, and attachments. The way we do one thing is the way we do all things, so I started letting go of the tangible stuff, and it opened the door to releasing the intangible as well.

Do you remember the magicians who used to spin plates atop poles on the stage at the circus? The trick was to get as many of the plates spinning at the same time without letting any of them drop. This required constant attention to each plate, giving it just enough momentum every few seconds to keep it spinning, and then rushing to do the same with another plate to keep it from falling off the pole. This depicts how most of us live our lives with multi-tasking condoned in the workplace and perpetuated in our society as an asset when it's actually a disease from which we are suffering in epidemic proportion (like we're addicted to being busy or something).

As a direct by-product of a "bigger, better, faster, more" mentality, we take a simple life and complicate it to no end. Our "wants" become "needs," and before we know it, we believe we can't live without something that we didn't even know existed a year ago. We are spoiled rotten, over stimulated, and rightfully exhausted, but it's our own fault. Some of the plates we try spinning don't even make sense with everything else we've got going on, so we essentially guarantee that one or more of them will inevitably drop. And we've been doing this for so long that we don't know any other way to be.

One trip to Hawaii was all it took to show me an alternative way to live, and it completely changed my life.

A good friend had moved to Oahu and invited me to visit. I'd been booking all of my boss's travel on my personal credit card for years, so I had accumulated enough mileage points to cover a free round-trip flight to the island. With plenty of vacation days available, free airfare, and a free place to stay while visiting, there was no reason for me not to go.

At first, I didn't understand why people considered Hawaii "paradise." There was constant traffic, potholes everywhere, cracked pavement, ugly balconies used as storage, and nothing new or modern, which I initially judged as sub-par and sometimes inadequate. But then, corny as it sounds, while sitting in traffic on the way back to town from the North Shore, I saw a bumper sticker on an old car that read, "Slow Down! This Ain't the Mainland!" and it hit me (not the car, an epiphany): I had been looking at the island through my

"Seattle eyes," so to speak, comparing everything I saw to how much "better" it was on the mainland, rather than observing everything without judgment to truly appreciate what was right in front of me.

So I started embracing the relaxed culture of the island, where nobody operated with any sense of urgency. While it seemed absurd at first, it made complete sense when I witnessed the relaxing effect it had on the people around me. Nothing was a "big deal"… what a concept!

By the second or third day on the island I had made friends who surfed or played volleyball every day after work. They would simply pull up next to the volleyball courts, change into their shorts, and play until the sun went down. The weather was always nice, so sometimes we even played tennis afterwards because the court lights stayed on 24 hours a day.

This went on for the two weeks I was there, during which nobody cared that I wasn't from the island, or that I wore the same pair of board shorts every day; they embraced me as one of their own and I immediately felt at home. I'll never forget Elena, who always brought treats to share with all of us on the court (papayas, mangoes, pineapple, lilikoi, guava… it was incredible; I had found paradise).

When the plane left Honolulu back to Seattle, and I watched the island of Oahu disappear behind me, I promised myself to head back there as soon as possible. I finally knew what kind of life I wanted to lead and where I wanted to live it, and nothing was going to stop me. I got home, rushed to the computer, and purchased another ticket to Hawaii for a few months down the road (I just had to know that I'd be back there at some point in the future).

Returning to the fluorescent-lit office after that vacation was excruciatingly painful. There I was, with a nice tan, remembering the feeling of sand between my toes, and I couldn't figure out why I was still working there. I mean, my debt was finally paid off, so what was I going to do with that "extra" $1,000 that I no longer needed to send to credit card companies each month? Luckily, the first thought I had was, "I guess I no longer have to make that 'extra' $1,000 every month; I can just quit this job, sell everything I own, and move to the island where I can work less and live more!"

The wheels were set into motion.

A couple of months later, I went back to Hawaii and seamlessly picked up where I had left off (playing volleyball with the same friends as if I had never left, swimming, walking around town, and eating at all my favorite local spots). The hiking trails were stunning, the weather was always perfect, and the pace of life was just right. I knew that the next time I flew there, it would be a one-way ticket.

I will never forget my first day back at work after that second trip to Hawaii. At exactly 3:00 p.m., everyone at the office slowly started moving toward the lunchroom, like cattle, for free cake and cookies because another paralegal was celebrating her 30-year anniversary at the firm.

Did you catch that? She was CELEBRATING thirty years of sitting in a cubicle under fluorescent lights! This was great for her, but it terrified me! I had already been working in the corporate world for ten years (five in the Bay Area and five in Seattle), and this "celebration" was a glimpse into my own future if I didn't make a change, and fast!

Without hesitation, I walked into my boss's office, closed the door, and just looked at him. I don't know if it was my dark tan or the look of terror in my eyes, but he just smiled and said, "You're moving to Hawaii, aren't you?"

He was incredibly supportive, and after five years of working so well together, I wasn't going to leave him high-and-dry with just a two-weeks' notice. I told him the wheels were in motion and that we ought to start taking the necessary steps to make the transition as smooth as possible. He admitted that if it weren't for his wife and four kids, he'd be doing the same thing himself (only he would head toward the mountains in Montana, not the islands, but same idea).

When it was time for me to leave the firm, the Human Resources Department tried everything they could to lure me into staying. They offered me what anyone in the corporate world would normally beg for: higher pay, more vacation, lighter workload, and schedule flexibility. This would have tempted me had I not already tasted the life I truly wanted. I declined their offer with tremendous gratitude, and I'm really glad I did.

As I said before, the dream, perhaps for all of us, is to lead a simple and uncomplicated life. And even though it's difficult to imagine a way out of our current situations if we feel "stuck," there are always options. The trick is to figure out what is standing in our way of deciding to get out. That "something" is almost always our own fears and insecurities.

My friends Jay and Martin are a great example of this. They are in similar positions: both are in their thirties, love to hike, camp, travel, and explore various cultures, cuisines, and music; and they both own a home.

For the past decade, Martin has been renting out his home and using that rental income to travel to more than thirty countries around the globe (and counting). He has had adventures that most people, including Jay, only dream about, while working random jobs here and there to supplement the money he makes from his rental unit. He never stays with any employer for too long (there are volcanoes to climb, after all, and remote islands to explore). He is truly living his life to the fullest every single day. I admire Martin's passion more than he realizes, and I love that he can embrace each moment without fear or concern, worry or reservation.

Like Martin, Jay also leases his house to tenants whose rent payment not only covers the mortgage but the rest of his living expenses as well. Unlike Martin, however, Jay has spent the last decade miserably working 60 hours a week (and complaining about it for just as long). Only after reading Buddhist Boot Camp was he inspired to work less in order to live more, but he's finding that his identity is too tightly weaved into his job title, so he's having a difficult time letting go.

It's easy for me to see that a life of leisure is clearly available to Jay right here and now (he technically doesn't have to work at all if he doesn't want to, and certainly not full time). Strangely enough, however, instead of deciding which of the spinning plates he could let fall in order to simplify his life, he is continually adding responsibilities (financial and otherwise), essentially complicating his own life even more.

He says the intention is to continue doing this "for just a little longer" so that his true dream can materialize five or ten years down the road (as if life comes with any guarantees that he'll even be here for that long), but what's even worse is that he already said the same thing five years ago.

Greed has Jay reaching for more, and fear keeps him from letting go of the past in order to be in the present. It all boils down to choices, and his actions clearly convey his priority is more money, not the leisurely life he claims to want but clearly not enough to do anything about it. Once I pointed this out to him (what are friends for?), he admitted that the addiction to the hustle-and-bustle and the attachment to having a work-related title, if only to impress his parents, are both stronger than his desire to live the simple life that he claims to want. He wouldn't have arrived at this clarity had he not honestly asked himself and answered, "If I want a stress-free life, then why do I keep making decisions that add more stress to my life?"

Whatever we want more will inevitably be what motivates us. When in doubt, look at your actions and you'll see your priorities. That's what helped Jay clearly see that he was more motivated by greed and fear than he was by love and faith.

Those who are afraid of never having enough, ultimately never have enough. And those who are grateful for what they already have, always live in abundance.

Whenever I think of Jay waiting to start living his life, the following quote from W.M. Lewis comes to mind: "The tragedy of life is not that it ends so soon, but that we wait so long to begin it."

When we have more
than enough, we don't
need to raise our
standard of living,
we need to raise our
standard of giving.

— 15 —

THE BEST THINGS IN LIFE

Moving to Hawaii was easy. I sold or donated everything I owned (from furniture to winter clothes), and took that one-way flight to the island with only a backpack and volleyball net. I hadn't saved any money, but I didn't owe anybody any money either, so I felt free!

Without a job lined up in Honolulu, or even a place to live, I was riding on so much faith that "optimistic" doesn't even begin to describe it. Arguably, "stupid" does a pretty good job of describing it as well (after all, there are more homeless people on Oahu per capita than anywhere else in the U.S.), but I was (and still am) convinced that making love-based decisions leads to everything in the universe conspiring to work in our favor, whereas fear-based decisions create unnecessary obstacles for us to overcome. So I vowed to always contemplate whether my decisions are love-based or fear-based, and to only make love-based decisions from that point forward. This eliminated worrying (which is sort of like praying for what you don't want), and opened the door to possibilities, not excuses.

The entire point of moving to the island was to lead a simple and uncomplicated life, right? So every decision had to be weighed to ensure it contributed to living the dream every day instead of postponing it to "maybe some day."

Looking for a part-time job was really easy. Every place was hiring: from hotels and grocery stores to coffee shops and restaurants. And because I'd worked such a great variety of part-time jobs on the side over the years (from doing graphic design and photography on the weekends to pulling graveyard shifts at gas stations or go-go-dancing at nightclubs, making sandwiches at Subway, or smoothies at Jamba Juice), now that I was in Hawaii, any job that didn't involve a cubicle and fluorescent lights was fine by me! After all, I really only needed to make enough to pay for food and half of the rent in a shared studio. Hawaii is one of the few states where employers give you health insurance if you work 20 hours a week (not 40), so even a part-time job at Starbucks would have been enough.

Luckily, a friend on the island found me a job managing an online art gallery for four hours a day, which I was eventually able to do from home because it was online. I worked during the hottest part of the day so that I could spend the rest of my time playing volleyball and tennis, swimming in the ocean, hiking, you name it.

I don't understand why people think living on the island is so expensive. All the stuff I enjoy doing doesn't cost a thing! Maybe it's expensive if you want to buy a house, drive a car, and have kids, but not if you want to get around town on a bike, enjoy nature, and make the most out of life. Perhaps that's why so many people are credited for saying, "The richest man is not he who has the most, but he who needs the least."

— 16 —

DOMINO EFFECT

I'm not sure how my intention to live a simple and uncomplicated life led to me taking the monastic vows and moving into a Buddhist monastery, but I guess it isn't too far of a stretch if you really think about it. When I told my best friend in Seattle that I was becoming a monk, her response was perfect! She said, "I'm shocked, but I'm not surprised!"

The decision to take the monastic vows came on the heels of ending a romantic relationship. I realized it was adding drama and complications to my life instead of enriching it.

When I made a list of the qualities I wanted to see in someone with whom I could imagine spending the rest of my life, the details of skin color, age, financial status, career of choice, and even gender, no longer mattered. I finally understood the importance of foregoing the shallow end of the list and looking for someone kind, generous, giving, forgiving, compassionate, unconditionally accepting, supportive, loving, honest, respectful, and trustworthy. It occurred to me, while making that list, that I was essentially describing God (as I understood her/him to be). And so it made sense for me to marry God, and to vow to be of service for the greater good.

The journey took me down a path of inquiries that led to the Dalai Lama. The first time I heard him speak, I was not expecting him to have such a youthful sense of humor and casual demeanor, so I liked him right away. I was so enthralled, in fact, that I thought my search was over. "That's it!" I exclaimed. "I will just become a Buddhist Monk, and.. 'poof,' ego-be-gone!"

I was ambitious but completely naive.

Keep in mind that by this point in my life I had already quit the corporate job, sold all of my belongings, and moved to an island in the most secluded populated spot on earth. Taking the monastic vows seemed like the most logical next step toward a simple life. I mean, nobody ever looks at monks and thinks, "Boy, their lives must be complicated!" Boring, maybe, but never complicated.

A quick glance at the monastic vows was very reaffirming. I had already adopted a vegetarian diet to minimize the harmful impact I might have on other beings; I hadn't had a drop of alcohol in a decade; I was actively fine-tuning my mindfulness and awareness skills (a lifelong practice); and I already considered the meditation cushion my "happy place," so a monk was already in the making.

There was one final hurdle for me to climb: sexually-charged thoughts that lead to sexually-charged actions. Luckily, this is addressed in the third Buddhist precept, which is beautifully translated by Thich Nhat Hanh in *For a Future to Be Possible*.

Even though I included his translation in my last book, I think it's important to share it here as well:

> "Aware of the suffering caused by sexual misconduct, I vow to cultivate responsibility and learn ways to protect the safety and integrity of individuals, couples, families and society. I am determined not to engage in sexual relations without love and a long-term commitment. To preserve the happiness of myself and others, I am determined to respect my commitments and the commitments of others. I will do everything in my power to protect children from sexual abuse and to prevent couples and families from being broken by sexual misconduct."

The third precept describes sexual responsibility, not celibacy, but after years of sexual addiction and abuse, asking me to be sexually responsible was like asking an alcoholic to drink responsibly; I didn't trust myself in that department, so complete abstinence was the ultimate solution to my life's remaining complications.

Just like someone who is trying to lose weight is better off not keeping junk food in the house, or why an alcoholic in recovery keeps a dry home, I knew this level of discipline was necessary for me to avoid temptation in order to stay focused.

There are many faces of obsessive behavior with which we all struggle to one degree or another. Whether it's overeating, binge drinking, compulsive exercising, sex, or anything that we do to "escape," many seeds of awareness and clarity can sprout into healthier patterns of behavior through humility.

In my twenties, I slept with anyone who found me attractive because I confused being attracted-to with being loved. Much like everybody else, I was hungry for intimacy and connection, acceptance and affection, but the more I slept around, the worse I felt.

Eventually I realized that I was hurting everyone around me by using them to make myself feel better, and failing miserably at that as well.

The third precept is a perfect example of what I love so much about Buddhism: there are no commandments or rules to follow, only suggestions and invitations to try different things in order to see if they work or not.

There is no, "Thou shalt not kill" commandment, either. The first precept reads, "Aware of the suffering caused by the destruction of life, I vow not to kill, not to let others kill, and not to condone any act of killing in the world through my thoughts, words, or actions." How beautiful is that? It simply invites us to contemplate the pain caused by the destruction of life, and asks us whether we want to contribute to that pain or opt out. I love it!

This explains why some Buddhists are vegetarians and some are not; the precepts are there for us to contemplate, interpret, and then apply as we understand them. There is no "wrong" answer; everything is subject to time, place, and circumstance.

Only after many years of celibacy did I finally understand the difference between using sex and abusing it, and that neither is a substitute for self-respect, love, confidence, or acceptance. Finding someone to love you is not a substitute for learning to love yourself.

I'm not suggesting that we all go without sex, but I think it's good to ask ourselves, "When I have sex, why am I having it?"

Your answer to that question may surprise you. For years I was having sex for all the wrong reasons: either because I felt like I had nothing else of value to offer, or to get validation from others because I lacked security and confidence in myself. It is only after we see divinity and absolute perfection in our own reflection that we can truly see it in others.

A friend of mine on a similar path called me crying one day, explaining how despite everything else going really well in her life (work was good; health was good; and her yoga, spiritual, and meditation practices were comforting, consistent, and balanced), she still found herself, every once in a while, craving the "weight of a man on top of her," as she explained it. "Not sex," she said, "just that physical closeness and connection."

When I hung up the phone I thought to myself, "How can I make sure that no matter how far I go down this monastic path, I don't still find myself lacking something like physical contact at the end of the day someday?" I couldn't bear the thought of possibly feeling like something was missing from my life instead of focusing on how rich it was.

As an experiment, I decided to apply the same logic to the this dilemma that I had applied in the past to smoking, drinking, and eating meat. At one point I stopped doing those things altogether, and after enough time had passed, they ceased to even cross my mind. So what would happen if I were to eliminate physical contact altogether? Would I ultimately lose interest in physical connection and therefore free myself from the craving and sense of emptiness that my friend was experiencing?

For over five years I abstained from any and all physical contact more intimate than handshakes (no hugs, no kisses, nothing beyond a fist-bump), and the experiment actually worked! Not only did I no longer find myself longing for physical connection, I became extremely aware of how much other people relied on it, needed it, and either used or abused it for various reasons.

The unexpected side effect of this experiment was that it forced me to redefine intimacy in non-physical terms: to be intimate without so much as a simple hug at my disposal.

One of the teachers at the monastery guided us through a sharing exercise, which I thought was extremely intimate: He had each of us sit cross-legged directly in front of someone we didn't know, and then he invited one person from each pair to ask the other participant a question. When the person across from us answered the question, we were instructed not to react to the answer they give nor discuss it any further, but to simply ask the question again. At the monastery, the questions were practice-specific, but you can imagine doing this exercise with a question like, "What are you angry about?"

We all have answers for most questions readily available in our back pockets, so to speak, and we are prepared to give those canned answers to anyone at a moment's notice. That's exactly the answer we each gave the first time a question was asked. And when the question was asked again, we all reached for our in-case-of-emergency backup answer. But when the question was asked a third, fourth, and fifth time, we had to really peel back the layers and dig deep to share from our core, which made all of us vulnerable, exposed, raw, radically honest, transparent and, more often than not, extremely uncomfortable.

When the person sitting across from me repeatedly asked why I chose to live at the monastery, I initially gave the expected response, "To learn," "To grow," or "To find peace." But when I finally arrived at the truth, I broke down crying and admitted there was a lot of fear behind my decision. I was afraid that if I couldn't fit-in at the monastery (after not being able to fit-in anywhere else), I might never find a place where I belong.

Once all of our "fronts" were dropped, we unearthed repressed memories, unexamined fears, insecurities and anxieties, and finally looked at ourselves (dark spots and all), sometimes for the first time ever.

It occurred to me that it's very easy to spend time with a friend, give them a hug, and share small talk, but it's not so easy to practice this level of radical honesty with one another even though it's extremely important and beneficial. In the long run, abstaining from physical contact with others and committing myself to this new level of intimacy instead, has proven to significantly strengthen my relationships with everyone in my life, not weaken it.

People often tell me that my honesty is an act of courage and bravery, but I don't see it that way. I have nothing to lose by being honest, and if we are to treat others the way we wish to be treated ourselves, then we must begin by breaking down the walls and barriers we constructed when we thought other people can hurt us. As we've already discovered, nobody can make us feel anything without our consent, so there's nothing to defend and nothing to protect.

When you think about it, nobody can hurt you by using information about you that you, yourself, accept. The key, therefore, is for all of us to be comfortable with who we are, not "despite our blemishes," but by realizing that we aren't marred in any way whatsoever.

So regardless of what you've done in the past, don't let it ruin your present or stand in the way of your future. John Lennon was so right when he said, "Being honest may not get you a lot of friends, but it will always get you the right ones."

— 17 —

COMPANIONSHIP

The experiment of abstaining from physical contact for a few years helped me discover this new, deeper level of intimacy. I'm not saying that physical contact is a bad thing, only that it's not the only way to be intimate with someone, as I discovered during my relationship with Marisa.

When I first met her, our compatibility was undeniable. We shared a mutual level of unconditional love, honesty, respect and trust for one another, which made living together an absolute pleasure. Our sole intention was to do whatever we could to make each other's life easier and more manageable, not to complicate it with demands or expectations. Marisa wasn't the reason for my happiness, nor was I hers, but we certainly enjoyed spending time together and figuring out creative ways to enrich each other's lives... it was so much fun!

I was taking a few college classes and working from home at the time, and Marisa worked in an office building nearby. Each morning we would meditate together for a few minutes, and then I would make juice for the both of us while she got ready for work. I packed her breakfast and lunch so that she wouldn't have to rush to the office or spend any money eating out, and depending on the day of the week, I either headed off to school or worked out of my home office.

On Saturdays, I played beach volleyball all day. Marisa knew I'd be famished when I got home, so she always had something delicious waiting for me in the kitchen. It was an absolute pleasure to do things for one another; and none of it was out of obligation, guilt, or duty. You should have seen her face light up with joy when I put extra ginger in our morning juice. Seeing her so happy was the highlight of my day!

In the evenings, Marisa would get home from work, quickly change into sweats and a T-shirt, and we would go on a short hike together before the sun set. We are both foodies who stick to a plant-based diet, so we had a lot of fun preparing dinner together. And before going to bed, we would take turns reading a chapter out loud to one another from Susan Trott's *The Holy Man.*

We would say goodnight to each other, and then Marisa would go into her bedroom, and I went into mine. It was the most ideal relationship I could imagine because as much as we loved spending time together, we also treasured our nights alone.

While I don't know if this relationship was so great because it was platonic, I can't help but think that it had something to do with it.

When we enter into a new relationship with someone, we each bring a blueprint of what we think it "should" look like instead of co-creating an ideal that best suits that specific relationship. Where does it say that a couple has to go to bed together at the same time each night, share a bank account, or have children? We must question where those ideas come from and whether they even apply to us. Most arguments stem from unexpressed expectations that go unsatisfied because of it.

Marisa and I respected each other's space, needs, and time, and demanded little to nothing from one another. Whether we went to parties, movies, restaurants, or road trips together, we managed to enhance each experience without taking anything away from it.

In a healthy relationship it's imperative, above all, to be supportive of one another. If your boyfriend decides to be a photographer, for example, your role would be to simply say, "Great! Let's go find you a camera, and if you need a model, I'm all yours!" And if six months later he changes his mind and says he wants to be a nurse, you are to say, "Great! Let's get you an application at the local nursing school, and I'll help you with your homework, if need be."

The only scenario in which it would be appropriate for you to discourage your partner from pursuing something is if they suddenly decide to do what goes against their own core values (not yours, mind you, theirs). If your girlfriend is an environmentalist, for example, and she gets a tempting job offer from a company she may or may not know is owned by a large fracking corporation, then it's appropriate for you to mirror back to her that her core values would make it really difficult to go to work every day, no matter how much money the company is offering.

The relationship with Marisa improved my communication skills and the way I relate to everyone in my life. She always said we meet people for a reason, a season, or a lifetime, so even though we eventually parted ways, I am forever grateful for our time together. As Eckhart Tolle said, "To love is to recognize yourself in another."

— 18 —

NON-ATTACHMENT

When I was clad in full monastic robes and free of worldly possessions, it finally happened: a monk was born (poor, celibate, solitary, and contemplative).

Remember how I thought this new direction would work like a magic potion to eliminate the ego? Well, that was before I realized that we aren't supposed to destroy the ego, per se, but to make peace with it instead. Monkhood, as it turned out, was not a magic potion at all; the work was just beginning.

We've all been told that if it looks like a duck, sounds like a duck, and walks like a duck, then it must be a duck, right? But that's not always the case. Wearing holy attire does not make a person holy. I have met many ego-driven priests at the monastery who had an aura of superiority about them because they had memorized some sutras and were proud of their chanting abilities. Many were actually inconsiderate, unkind, and rude. Tyler Durden was right once again: "Sticking feathers up your butt does NOT make you a chicken!"

Tyler Durden, by the way, is a fictional character in *Fight Club*, written by Chuck Palahniuk. I would say that I'm quoting Chuck when I quote Tyler, but while on the topic of ego and one's alter-ego, Tyler does what the narrator never would, and vice versa. So I think of Chuck as the narrator of Tyler's thoughts. And *Fight Club*, much like our own spiritual journey, "is not a weekend retreat. It's not a seminar. So stop trying to control everything and just let go. Let go!"

When the time was right, I decided to keep the vows but to let go of the monastic robes. Inside the monastery, the robes made perfect sense (we all had the same haircut and clothes, which literally conveyed that we're all the same, interconnected, and equal). But outside the monastery, the robes separated me from others as different and maybe even "special," conveying the opposite message of what I intended. I knew the robes had to go when an old lady on the bus offered me her seat.

My belief is that we are all one, so it doesn't make sense for my clothes to contradict that. It was my own teachers who asked me, "Why the robes, Timber? Why can't you just be the guy in town with the bright eyes?"

— 19 —

LETTING GO

A good friend of mine recently ended an on-again off-again relationship. You know... months of breaking up and getting back together, only to break up again and repeat the cycle. But he swore that this time it was "final."

He called me a few days later and said, "Part of me wants to try again," and that's exactly the problem he needed to address. If only "a part of him" wants to go back, that's not enough. I mean, a part of me wants to join the Peace Corps while another part of me wants to move back into the monastery. There is a part of me that wants to drink, smoke, and party again for the first time in over a decade, just like a part of me wants to slap certain people upside the head every once in a while. I don't do any of those things, of course, and that's because only a part of me wants to do them, not all of me. Every aspect of my being must first be in agreement with what I'm about to do, or I choose not to do it at all.

Relationships are tough because chemistry does not necessarily determine compatibility. Our primary relationship in life is with ourselves, so we need to make sure we don't create internal conflict by only listening to "a part" of ourselves. Harmonious agreement between who we are and the kind of person we want to be is essential for inner peace; only then would our actions be in line with our values.

In order for our behavior to align with our core beliefs, we must be willing to let go of anything that gets in our way (be it ego, anger, resentment, or fear). "Letting go" is everywhere in Buddhist lingo, and it makes perfect sense why. But how do we let go of ego or fear? Any attempt to destroy either one just gives it more energy to grow. But learning to make peace with the ego, acknowledging it while deciding not to act on its behalf, is the way to end the internal conflict. It may sound obvious, but the best way to win the war is to not fight it.

Conquering fear is a little different, because to do so we simply need to feed our faith, and the fear will die on its own. Any attention we give to fear only reaffirms it. Making only love-based decisions solves this problem.

To feed our faith, we must wholeheartedly trust that everything will be okay no matter what (your definition of "okay" may need to change). You can start by noticing when you're about to make a fear-based decision, and simply not make it (or if fear stops you from making a decision, don't let it).

Was I scared to move to Hawaii without a job lined up or a place to live? Of course I was! But I did it anyway. That's the practice: acknowledge the fear but don't be scared of it.

Everything I'm talking about (letting go of ego, feeding our faith so that our fears starve to death, and moving forward in life with full conviction instead of hesitation), may sound easier said than done on the surface, but as challenging as all that may be, it's still easier than living the rest of our lives fueled by fear.

How we identify ourselves must be fluid and flexible instead of rigid and unbending. Like everybody else on this planet, I am a lot of things, but not one of them defines me.

If we are stubborn and insist on a solid identity, then we're blocking our own potential for growth and resisting the continuous flow of life. The added danger of seeing ourselves as one solid thing is that we then look at others as only one thing as well, which overlooks everything else they might be.

As you already know, I often draw inspiration from empowering quotes that beautifully encapsulate a great idea into something short and easy to digest. The messenger, as far as I'm concerned, is irrelevant; it's the message that has power. But time and time again, whenever I quote Mother Teresa, for example, people criticize my choice because of some terrible things that she may or may not have done, as if any of those things negate the wonderful work she's demonstrated in the world.

The purpose of continually contemplating our answer to the question "Who am I?" is to stay open-minded about ALL the things we are. Then we wouldn't be so quick to label others.

The fact that I still have a long way to go does not diminish the value of how far I have already traveled. We have all been lied-to, cheated-on, overworked, underpaid, wronged, misunderstood, and under-appreciated, yet we're still here. We are not broken. We can even be wronged again and still keep going, so long as we don't identify as victims.

Nothing has ever happened TO us, everything happens FOR us (for us to learn from, grow from, and, most importantly, move on from).

May we never criticize what we haven't even made the effort to understand, for once we understand, there is nothing left to criticize. You can go ahead and quote me on that!

— 20 —

CLIFFHANGER

One year, on April 22nd, in celebration of Earth Day, I went to my favorite surfing spot on Oahu to pay my respect to one of Mother Nature's greatest masterpieces: the ocean. The waves were bigger than they had been in a very long time, and I couldn't wait to dive-in and wrap myself in her embrace. She's powerful, unpredictable, immense, strong, and she demands respect. I was foolish, irresponsible, cocky, and practically asking for a wake up call... and let me tell you: she set me straight!

Getting tossed around in her waves wasn't a problem; I thoroughly enjoyed it, actually, and I couldn't get enough. Climbing back up the cliff, however, was a bit of a challenge, especially with waves as enormous as they were that day (many regularly die or get seriously injured trying to get out).

Only halfway up the side of the mountain, I realized that I couldn't possibly make it to the top shelf before the next wave crashes into the reef. When this happened in the past, I had always managed to push myself off the rocks and back into the water before trying to climb out again because I had enough time; but on that day, the next wave did not only hit faster than expected, it was also much larger than the ones before it.

Clinging to the side of the cliff, with the shelf still three or four feet above me, and the water swiftly moving away from me (three, six, and now twelve feet below me) I didn't have enough time to climb out nor push myself far enough away from the wall and into the water.

Knowing exactly what was about to happen, my mind sorted through a lifetime of information at an unbelievable rate. It was like a computer program running a script faster than anything yet invented, and the solution to my predicament flashed before my eyes in big, bold, red letters. Like the numerals on a digital clock, it flashed with great urgency and a buzzing sound similar to what you'd hear from an alarm clock, and all it said was, LET GO.

I closed my eyes, released my grip, and fell into the next wave like a rag doll. The ocean swell immediately lifted me up, slammed me into the mountain, and dragged me against the reef. It felt like I was in a washing machine lined with razor blades. I was spinning, tumbling, and tossed around without a clue as to which way was up or down. Lost in foam one minute with a deafening thunder-like roar, and deeply submerged below the surface the next, all sound was muted in a big blur, and ocean water was stinging my eyes as I searched for some point of reference to reorient myself.

The benefits of meditation aren't necessarily apparent during our 30 minutes on the cushion every day (pleasant as they may be), but they become clear later in the day, when we need to keep our minds focused, clear, and calm, regardless of external stimuli. If your nose itches while you sit, for example, you don't scratch it; you just observe and notice: my nose is itchy... interesting. If it feels like your foot is falling asleep, you don't move or massage it; you just observe and notice: my foot's asleep... interesting. The intention is to introduce a gap between impulse and action. And if we can do it in meditation, we will be better equipped to do it in real life situations that call for a calm and collected perspective (and what situation doesn't?)

As the wave continued to slam me into the wall, my awareness narrated the experience to me as it was happening: I just broke my leg against the rock... interesting. The reef just slashed me across my back... interesting. I need to take a breath but I can't, because if I do, I will swallow ocean water and that's how people drown. Oh.. drowning... that's what's happening... I'm drowning. That's interesting... I've never done that before; let's see what that's like.

The narration was oddly calm. It felt like I was watching this near-death incident happening to someone else on TV. I was observing it with curiosity, not judgment. It was surreal. As soon as I released my grip from the cliff and fell back into the water, I didn't just physically let go, I completely surrendered to the moment. Just like in meditation, I didn't resist, reject, or fight what was happening. I remained calm and observant; it was fantastic.

When there seemed to be no end in sight to all the tumbling and turning, I figured this was the ultimate moment to which everyone is bound, but I didn't panic; I was actually curious what death was going to be like. After all, I've never done that before either, and it would be interesting to finally experience what all the fuss was about.

Just when I completely surrendered to that moment, my head poked out of the water like a buoy, and I saw two surfers looking shocked at my sudden appearance out of nowhere. I yelled, "I need a board!" and they lifted me onto theirs, noticing immediately that I was slashed, dripping blood, with a bone sticking out of my leg, but I was smiling the way people do at the end of a rollercoaster ride. I couldn't believe I'd survived!

The surfers carried me out and ran up the hill to find my friend and his pickup truck. A neighbor nearby saw it happen and immediately came out of his house to hose me down. My friend got directions from him to the nearest hospital, and then threw me in the back of his pickup. There was loose, flapping flesh and blood squirting everywhere, so it made sense to keep me out of the cabin. He drove me to what we thought was the nearest hospital, and he ran in to get me a wheelchair, put me in it, and rolled me into the waiting room of what was actually a pediatric clinic; there were kids EVERYWHERE!

The nurses immediately jumped into action and opened the door for my friend to wheel me to the back as quickly as possible so that nobody had to see me in that condition for longer than necessary. If there was one moment out of the entire incident during which I panicked, this was it. The adults in the waiting room either averted their eyes or winced if they looked at me for too long, but right before I made it through the door, I made eye contact with a little girl, maybe 4 or 5 years old, who was sitting on her mom's lap, and she simply raised her hand to wave at me, and said, "Hi!!!!"

That moment calmed me down in a flash. To that little girl, I was just another kid with a boo-boo who simply needed to see the doctor. There was absolutely no judgment in her greeting, and I just smiled back, raised my bloody hand, said "Hi!" right back to her, and waved hello.

The doctor said they weren't equipped to take care of me at the clinic, but they could clean me up to be driven to a real hospital for better care. He asked me why I was in such a great mood, and I just smiled and said, "Are you kidding?! I'm alive!"

The nurse cleaned my wounds and apologized profusely for causing me pain, and all I could do was smile and say, "It's okay. This [pointing to my body] is temporary; you're doing a great job!"

At the hospital to which I was later transferred, a nurse named Nikki changed my bandages every day, and because I couldn't really use my hands or feet for a while, I had a lot of time to meditate and think about the incident.

There was an important lesson for me to learn from that experience, and I was going to figure out what it was.

In the year that this happened, I was still wearing the monastic robes. My epiphany was that it was silly of me to think that the robes (now speaking figuratively) could "come off" when it's inconvenient to wear them, and then put back on when I'm ready. The robes are never to be taken off (again, figuratively), as they represent my vows, which are to never be taken lightly or treated like a part-time job. This was a full-time commitment to be of service to others, so I needed to leave my days of jumping off cliffs and thrill-seeking behind.

After my epiphany, Nikki came in to change my bandages the way she had done every day, and we were both shocked to find absolutely no traces of blood or even scabs from the recent injuries. All my wounds had completely healed as if they had either never occurred, or, in the case of the beautiful scar across my back, as if they had happened a really long time ago.

Now that I have no fear of death, I am more intrigued by it than scared. Not intrigued enough to seek it out, mind you, but enough to be excited about the day it arrives.

I think Dan Millman explained it best when he said, "Death is a transformation. It's a little more radical than puberty, but nothing to get particularly upset about."

— 21 —

READY

Death is something that people rarely discuss, and when they do, it's always with tremendous discomfort. The mystery of death intrigues me more than it frightens me, so I always approach the topic with great curiosity.

With the risk of sounding insensitive yet again, what baffles me is that people's reaction to receiving the news of death is almost always shock. It's the one thing in the world that we know to expect, yet we are rarely ever prepared for it. And one of the reasons we aren't prepared for it is because we avoid thinking or talking about it at all cost.

When a family member battles an ailment for many years and the rest of the family makes peace with their loved one's impending death, then it's not so traumatic for them. In fact, they often admit to feeling a sense of relief, and I think it's because they've been preparing for it for a long time. So what's stopping us from doing the same thing? We all have a terminal disease called life, and it's rather foolish to pretend otherwise.

A few years ago I was staying with my best friend to help her sell her personal belongings online so that she could put her house on the market, sell it, and travel for a while. She has always been somewhat of a hypochondriac (there is always something wrong with her and some new holistic way to cure it), and all of her friends and family have simply grown to accept this.

She lived by a very strict and rigid routine. She would wake up at the exact same hour every day, have two glasses of water with her morning dose of vitamins, and then head out for her daily class of hot yoga.

While I was staying with her, I slept in the loft upstairs, so I always heard the water running when she got up to brush her teeth, the kitchen drawer sliding open when she took her vitamins, the front door opening and closing when she left the house, and the sound of her footsteps slowly fading as she walked to the yoga studio.

One morning, as I lay awake in bed watching the rising sun cast growing shadows across the room, I sensed that something was different. It was right around the time my friend would normally follow her morning routine, yet I couldn't hear any of the usual sounds coming from downstairs. An hour later, there was still no movement below, so I mentally ran through all the possible scenarios for this morning unfolding differently than all the others. I'm no pessimist, so I didn't immediately entertain the idea of her dying during the night; I first considered a few other explanations for that morning's unusual silence. But then

I did think to myself, what if she DID die during the night? What would I do?

I sat up in bed, closed my eyes, and mentally walked down the stairs to discover her lifeless body lying on the bed. I checked to see if she was breathing, and when I discovered that she wasn't, I calmly walked out of the room, called 9-1-1, and told them what I had found. I then called her sister so she could notify the rest of the family, making it a point to remain calm through it all. Granted, it was easy to stay calm because I was just imagining the whole thing, but that triggered a series of similar experiments that I've been doing ever since: preparing for a phone call announcing my dad's death, imagining a cancer diagnosis from my doctor, and even following Thich Nhat Hanh's advice to lay very still on the floor in corpse pose, imagining my own body in the ground.

My friend overslept, by the way, because she had a difficult time falling asleep the night before; she was fine.

None of my experiments were done with morbid infatuation, mind you, I did them to eliminate the potential of being unprepared, shocked, or emotionally reactive when the real news of my father's death arrives, for example, and to make peace with my own mortality.

I understand, as I write this, that despite my intentions not to sound morbid, it's difficult to avoid. "Morbid," by definition, means "an unhealthy interest in disturbing and unpleasant events, such as death." But what I'm suggesting is a healthy interest in it (if that makes any sense).

I guess Mark Twain was right. "The fear of death follows from the fear of life. A man who lives his life fully is prepared to die at any time."

If you don't heal from

what hurt you,

you will end up bleeding on

people who didn't cut you.

— 22 —

CHOICES

Each decision we make throughout the day renders our next decision more difficult to make (it's called Decision Fatigue). And while most of us complain that our lives are too stressful and complicated, we don't fully grasp our personal responsibility for making it that way.

After imagining my life as an obstacle course (with its inherent mountains to climb, mud piles to run through, and strength endurance exercises to overcome), I asked myself two questions: am I unknowingly adding unnecessary challenges to an already complex design? Is there any way for me to simplify the process?

Have you ever stared at a restaurant's extensive menu and felt overwhelmed by the abundance of choices? Or stood in front of a closet full of clothes and felt like you had nothing to wear? That's because it's easier for us to make decisions when there are fewer options from which to choose. As a minimalist, I'm a big fan of making a single decision that makes all of my future decisions for me (for only as long as it makes sense, of course).

For example: preparing the same nutritious breakfast every day eliminates my having to worry about what to eat each morning. And by shaving my head once a week, I've done away with having to worry about what I look like (not to mention time and money saved on haircuts and products). The simplicity of owning only one pair of jeans and five gray T-Shirts is liberating. And by making the one-time decision to avoid eating anything fried or animal-derived, I've eliminated the possibility of ever being torn by too many options of what or where to eat.

Some people think what I do is absurd, but that's because we've been systematically programmed to secure a closet full of outfits, for example, and for everyone to abide by the same rules. Most people play along because they care what other people think about them, but other people's approval is not desired nor required, at least not by me. What other people think about me is none of my business.

This lifestyle is designed to not only avoid Decision Fatigue, but also to ensure our continued progression on a path that we've chosen for ourselves, regardless of inevitable temptations to stray. In the same way that I have fashioned a simple wardrobe and hairstyle, I have also written down my core values to use as a moral compass in every situation. Never am I torn about whether it's okay to kill (be it a spider or a neighbor), because I've taken a blanket vow not to contribute to the destruction of life (at least to the extent that I am able). There are no ethical dilemmas or moral challenges about how I ought to behave in any given situation, because in addition to taking the time to write down my core values, I've also written a paragraph describing the kind of person I want to be: kind, patient, giving, forgiving, accepting, calm, collected, and so on. I don't have to keep making a decision as to whether or not I ought to forgive this person or that one, for example, because I've already decided that I want to be the kind of person who forgives anyone for anything. And when we live in line with our values, following love instead of fear, and faith instead of doubt, we eliminate the potential for internal conflict, and ensure inner peace. As Gandhi said, "Happiness is when what you think, what you say, and what you do, are all in alignment."

The power behind this exercise is that we invite ourselves to live up to our highest potential. It works better than trying to live up to standards set for us by somebody else, because we generally don't like other people telling us what to do. In fact, when somebody else dictates a set of rules for us to follow (be it the Ten Commandments or the Constitution), we have a tendency to look for ways to break the rules, not follow them.

I propose that each of us writes down our own values as well as a paragraph describing the kind of person we want to be, and then cross-reference it with the kind of person we currently are. You will immediately see where you have some work to do.

I often say, "Your beliefs don't make you a better person, your behavior does," which confuses some people because they think our behavior is a by-product of our beliefs, but that's not always the case; you may believe that lying is wrong, for example, yet do it all the time. I think we need to close the gap between what we believe and how we act in the world.

Everything I've been talking about is connected to everything else: letting go of the condo and the sports-car made it easier to let go of my attachment to my image and status, which made letting go of insecurities, fears, and the ridiculous need to be accepted by others not only possible, but easy. So when I talk about letting go of religion to embrace God, I'm not suggesting we abandon our moral responsibility or accountability, but that we focus on being Christ-like instead of Christian, for example, or even Buddha-like instead of Buddhist.

Just imagine how liberating it would be to let go of anger, resentment, jealousy, pride, and your fear of death. Better yet, imagine letting go of everything that no longer serves you.

Now imagine embracing the mystery, letting go of your need to know, and being faithfully religionless: open-heartedly accepting everything under the sun, and joyously celebrating all of life's moments without any judgment.

As soon you lose the habitual tendency to label anything as "right" or "wrong," you'll be completely free to spread your wings like the image on the cover of this book, and fly unrestricted, unbound, unaffiliated, and uninhibited.

As Kris Kristofferson wrote, and Janis Joplin beautifully sang, "Freedom is just another word for nothing left to lose!"

— 23 —

ALLOW

It seems every experience in my life has prepared me for the next (even though I didn't know it at the time). Some of the skills I learned from working at the law firm proved to be useful when I managed the online art gallery a few years later; and lessons learned from previous relationships have significantly improved my communication skills in every relationship since. That's why I don't consider them "failed relationships" but successful ones; each served an important purpose.

Every obstacle, challenge, difficulty, and heartbreak has actually enriched my life, not damaged it. Perhaps that's why so many people say that learning is a gift, even when pain is your teacher.

There is a long list of things I don't know, and at the very top of that list is whether or not I will be alive five minutes from now. This does not prevent me from making plans to hike with my friend Kim in a couple of months, or dream of backpacking through New Zealand with my buddy Zach at some point in the future; not because I somehow know that this will happen, but because I trust that it will; I have faith.

Some people turn away from religion because of a negative experience at church, while for others the dogma of conditional acceptance finally hit too close to home. In order for religion not to make itself extinct, it needs to quickly evolve from being exclusive to inclusive. But as we've discovered, we don't need religion to be ethical or to have a relationship with God.

There are some wonderful churches doing great work in the world, alleviating suffering, and helping us in our time of need. I feel bad that many of them are losing credibility through no fault of their own. It's unfortunate that the good religious organizations with open doors to everyone are badly tainted by the extremists and fundamentalists who still preach judgment and hatred. Like the boy who cried "wolf," religion has given us too many false predictions, and because so many wars have started in the name of religion, the word "religious" is now somewhat of a derogatory term.

Fortunately, it's very possible to have a personal relationship with God without any religious affiliation, nor any association with a specific church or sect. I don't know about you, but my God loves everybody!

My faith is simple and doctrine-free. It is not a product of scientific research, a vision, or intuition; it is a direct result of multiple personal experiences where everything in the past happened for a reason that was simply far beyond my comprehension at the time. I think Jill Bolte Taylor said it best: "My spirituality is an intellectual process."

I'm not saying that some entity or deity has set a predetermined path for me to follow, nor that anything is "written in the stars." I'm simply comfortable admitting that I don't know why certain things happen or why they don't. The freedom derived from letting go of that compulsive need to know is pure bliss. It's not ignorance (which is a lack of attainable knowledge); it's faith: pure acceptance that some things cannot be known.

I don't get stressed if there is heavy traffic on my way into town or if I take the wrong exit, run out of gas, or even get into a fender bender. That's not because I believe some powerful force in the universe caused these things to happen in order to save me from a deadly accident that I might have gotten into had I left the house five minutes earlier or taken the usual route. I simply know that stressing about it doesn't solve anything! I trust that just like everything in the past has benefited my present, any experience is apparently necessary for me to have because it will likely benefit me in the future. It isn't necessary for me to understand why. I simply have faith.

So when I feel anxiety or tension about something that's about to happen, the mantra I quietly repeat to myself is "Allow."

And when I hyper-focus on the violence in the world, injustice, cruelty, or what I deem "unfair" from my very limited point of view, the mantra I quietly repeat to myself is "Zoom Out."

If my fists are clenched or my jaw is tight, I know it's because I'm clinging to an idea with rigidity and self righteousness, so the mantra I quietly repeat to myself is "Let Go."

I don't think God is "out there" somewhere, waiting to judge us on how well or poorly we've lived our lives. I believe God resides within each of us, and that when we serve others, give, forgive, accept, allow, zoom out, let go, and treat others with kindness, generosity, gratitude, compassion, and empathy, we are acting out of the God-ness in our hearts, the goodness within, which feels like heaven right here on earth.

Also within each of us, sitting right next to God, is our precious and obnoxious little ego. And every self-serving, unkind, greedy, inconsiderate, shallow, hurtful, pompous, unforgiving, and ungrateful thought, word, or action, stems from that ego. Trying to serve the ego or fill its endless desires can feel like hell right here on earth.

That's why each day I wake up and say, "Good morning" to both the God and the ego within me, and then take a couple of minutes to explain to the ego, as I would to a child, why despite hearing everything it desires for itself, I'm going to follow the God within me instead. At first, my ego used to throw a tantrum and get angry, but it has gotten used to it by now. Deflated, it just sits there waiting for an opportunity to pounce, but I find that the ego doesn't stand a chance as long as I keep my focus on God.

I know this is just a story that I tell myself because it enriches my life as well as the lives of everyone around me. But what's the alternative? To tell myself a story that fills me with fear, shame, or regret? No thanks; I like my reality. As Albert Einstein said, "Reality is merely an illusion, albeit a very persistent one." So why not choose to live in a reality that is positive and uplifting?

We've already discovered that what happens in our minds impacts our lives a whole lot more than anything else, and if our minds are capable of seeing the beauty in everything and everyone in the world, then why not do it?

As Mahatma Gandhi said, "If you do not see God in the next person you see, you need look no further."

Thank you for walking beside me on this journey. I appreciate you more than you could ever know.

Your Faithfully Religionless brother,
Timber Hawkeye

Namaste.

The Divine in me
acknowledges and honors
the Divine in you.

Also by Timber Hawkeye:

BUDDHIST BOOT CAMP

When I left the corporate world and moved to Hawaii, I started emailing my friends and family a short letter each month to let them know what's going on in my life. About eight years later, my friend Kim suggested that I share those emails on a blog (simply because she found the letters inspirational, and she figured that other people would benefit from reading them as well). And as it turns out, Kim was right! The blog became a book published by *HarperCollins*, and many people found the simple message in those emails refreshing, inspirational, and even more importantly, motivational.

I say motivation is more important because inspiration without action is just entertainment, and my invitation is for us to go beyond thinking that something is a "good idea" to actually implementing it into our daily lives.

The chapters in Buddhist Boot Camp can be read in any order, and are short and easy to understand. Each story and inspirational quote offers mindfulness-enhancing techniques that anyone can relate to, reinforcing what we intuitively know but have somehow forgotten.

Following is the introduction from the book along with a few sample chapters to give you a taste. Enjoy!

SAMPLE FROM
BUDDHIST BOOT CAMP

To make a long story short . . .

I sat there in front of the Tibetan Lama, wearing my maroon robes after years of studying Buddhism. "With all due respect," I said, "I don't believe the Buddha ever intended for his teachings to get THIS complicated!"

My teacher looked around at all the statues of deities with multiple arms and chuckled, "The Buddha didn't do this! The Tibetan culture did; this is their way. Why don't you try Zen? I think you would like it!"

So I bowed out of the temple, took off my robes, and moved into a Zen monastery far from home. Zen was simpler; that much was true (the walls were blank and I loved it), but the teachings were still filled with all the dogma that sent me running from religion in the first place.

There are many incredible books out there that cover all aspects of religion, philosophy, psychology and physics, but I was looking for something less "academic," so to speak. I was looking for something inspirational that people today would not only have the attention span to read all the way through, but actually understand and also implement in their daily lives. I pictured a simple guide to being happy, and in it just two words: "Be Grateful."

Gratitude has a way of turning what we have into enough, and that is the basic idea behind Buddhist Boot Camp.

The short chapters convey everything I have learned over the years in a way that is easy to understand, without you needing to know anything about Buddhism ahead of time. In fact, this book is not about being a Buddhist; it's about being a Buddha.

It is very possible (and perfectly okay) for someone who is Catholic, Muslim, Atheist or Jewish, for example, to still find the Buddha's teachings inspirational. You can love Jesus, repeat a Hindu mantra, and still go to temple after morning meditation. Buddhism is not a threat to any religion; it actually strengthens your existing faith by expanding your love to include all beings.

"Boot Camp" is a training method, and Buddhism is all about training the mind. Many people claim they don't have time to meditate every morning, but they still want spiritual guidance without any dogma or rituals attached. That is exactly what Buddhist Boot Camp provides in this quick and easy-to-digest format.

You are now a soldier of peace in the army of love; welcome to Buddhist Boot Camp!

Love is the Recognition of Beauty

A flower doesn't stop being beautiful just because somebody walks by without noticing it, nor does it cease to be fragrant if its scent is taken for granted. The flower just continues to be its glorious self: elegant, graceful, and magnificent.

Our Mother Nature has provided us with these immeasurably valuable teachers that blossom despite their short lifespan, stars that continue to shine even if we fail to stare at them, and trees that don't take it personally if we never bow down in gratitude for the oxygen they provide.

We also have an incredible and unlimited capacity to love, but the question is: can we do it like a flower? Without needing to be admired, adored, or even noticed? Can we open our hearts completely to give, forgive, celebrate, and joyfully live our lives without hesitation or need for reciprocity?

It seems like sometimes we go beyond taking things personally and are noticeably deflated when unappreciated. In-fact, devastated, we wilt in sorrow and then attempt to guard ourselves by withholding, using all sorts of protections and defenses. We get hurt (even angry), if our boss fails to recognize an astonishing feat, if a lover pulls their hand away, or when a friend forgets our birthday.

Can you imagine a flower copping an attitude for not being praised, or the moon dimming its glow because we're too self-absorbed to notice it more often?

Make an effort to shine no matter what, to love unconditionally, and to be a kind and gentle soul (even when nobody is watching).

And, if you're so inclined, hug the next tree you see and say, "Thank you!"

> *Everything has its beauty,*
> *but not everyone can see it.*
> — Confucius

What a Healthy Relationship Looks Like

Relationships are often misunderstood to be a simple commitment between two people; a dedication to each other with a sense of belonging to one another. Unfortunately, that kind of limited perspective breeds expectations, possessiveness and disappointment, and it reeks of ownership, greed, ignorance, and selfish desire.

A healthy relationship is an agreement between two people to support each other's spiritual practice. It is a vow to encourage each other's dedication, devotion and path, free from attachment or expectations (yet full of caring and compassion). A healthy relationship is based on unconditional love, not one where your need is to possess. Although you put plenty of "heart" into it, you lose nothing by giving it away. If each person is equally dedicated to inspire, create, awaken and enrich the lives of others, then there is no hidden agenda. It is far less important what one receives from the other as what one can give. Intimacy would suddenly surpass warmth and tenderness to also include patience, vulnerability, honesty, active listening, understanding, connection, and unwavering trust.

There is a healing power inherent in this kind of union, and it is capable of deep transformation for both people. It is an incredible opportunity to actually practice what you learn (from non-violent communication to meditation, listening, mirroring, authenticity, resolve, radical honesty, appreciation, purpose, equality, celebration, and mutuality).

A healthy relationship is a collaboration of sorts: two peaceful warriors spiritually supporting one another on their individual journeys to spread positivity and light.

May we all close the gap between what we believe and how we act in the world.

> *Love does not consist in gazing at each other,*
> *but in looking outward together*
> *in the same direction.*
> — Antoine de Saint-Exupéry

A Simple Life

My dad told me this story when I was a little kid, and even though many of us have heard it before (it was originally told by Heinrich Böll), I believe it deserves to be regularly shared, especially at every high school graduation around the world.

One summer, many years ago, a banker was vacationing in a small village on the coast. He saw a fisherman in a small boat by the pier with a handful of fish that he had just caught. The businessman asked how long it took him to catch the fish, and the man said he was out on the water for only a couple of hours.

"So why didn't you stay out there longer to catch more fish?" asked the businessman.

The fisherman said he catches just enough to feed his family every day, and then comes back.

"But it's only 2 p.m.!" said the banker, "What do you do with the rest of your time?"

The fisherman smiled and said, "Well, I sleep late every day, then fish a little, go home, play with my children, take a nap in the afternoon, then stroll into the village each evening with my wife, relax, play the guitar with our friends, laugh and sing late into the night. I have a full and wonderful life."

The banker scoffed at the young man, "Well, I'm a businessman from New York! Let me tell you what you should do instead of wasting your life like this! You should catch more fish to sell to others, and then buy a bigger boat with the money you make so you can catch even more fish!"

"And then what?" asked the fisherman. The banker's eyes got all big as he enthusiastically explained, "You can then buy a whole fleet of fishing boats, run a business, and make a ton of money!"

"And then what?" asked the fisherman again, and the banker threw his hands in the air and said, "You'd be worth a million! You can then leave this small town, move to the city, and manage your enterprise from there!"

"How long would all this take?" asked the fisherman. "Fifteen to twenty years!" replied the banker.

"And then what?"

The banker laughed and said, "That's the best part. You can then sell your business, move to a small village, sleep late, fish a little, play with your kids, take naps in the afternoon, go for an evening stroll with your wife after dinner, relax, sing, and play the guitar with your friends. You would have a full and wonderful life!"

The sherman smiled at the banker, quietly gathered his catch, and walked away.

Live simply so that others may simply live.
—Gandhi

Grasping

Just as we habitually hoard old birthday cards and souvenirs, bank statements and receipts, clothes, broken appliances and old magazines, we also hang on to pride, anger, outdated opinions and fears.

If we're so attached to tangible things, imagine how difficult letting go of opinions must be (let alone opening our minds to new ideas, perspectives, possibilities and futures). Our beliefs inevitably solidify to be the only truth and reality that we know, which puts a greater distance between us and anyone whose beliefs are different. This distance not only segregates us, it feeds our pride.

All of this grasping, by the way, stems from fear.

Why are we so terrified of change, strangers, the new or the unknown? Has the world not continually shown us beauty, sincerity and love through every generation? Are we so focused on the darkness that we no longer see or even remember the light? This is like *The NeverEnding Story*, if you remember it, wherein the minute people stop believing in a reality, it ceases to exist.

Love is real, people! And it's all around us. It vibrates beneath every act of kindness, service, art and family.

Fear is also very real; it permeates every doubt, despair, hesitation, hatred, jealousy, anger, pride and deceit.

Habitually contemplate whether your thoughts stem from love or from fear. If your thoughts originate in love, then follow them. But if they originate from a place of fear, then dig deep to find the root of your fear. Only then will you be able to finally let go of it so that fear no longer limits your possibilities.

There's nothing to complain about, no reason to be afraid, and everything is possible if we live FOR each other.

As far as I'm concerned, anything not meant to benefit others is simply not worth undertaking.

> *All the happiness in the world*
> *stems from wanting others to be happy,*
> *and all the suffering in the world*
> *stems from wanting the self to be happy.*
> —Shantideva

Less is More

My dad wanted to see what my life was like after years of hearing me talk about simplifying and being a minimalist. I told him that to TRULY understand it, he'd have to come live with me for a month, so he did.

He is very much the materialistic consumer, so when he first walked into my little apartment he said, "OMG! You don't have anything!"

After living with me for a month, however, preparing my meals with me, going for long walks every day, reading, writing, meeting with people one-on-one, and truly tasting the simplicity of my life, he hugged me before boarding his flight back home and said, "There is nothing missing from your life!"

It brought tears to my eyes because he actually got it. Both his statements were true: I don't have anything (in the materialistic sense), yet there is nothing missing from my life.

When I shared this particular story on Buddhist Boot Camp's Facebook page, I received hundreds of wonderful comments from readers who truly understood the significance of that moment with my dad.

Working part-time so that I can live full-time is the best decision I've ever made. I don't feel like I have "sacrificed" a life of "luxury"; I've simply exchanged material goods and the illusion of abundance for actual, true bliss.

I moved apartments every six months when I was younger, so I learned not to keep ANYTHING that I would later have to pack. No knickknacks, no souvenirs, no "stuff."

It feels great to be so light and free from any attachment to things. But if you're torn about throwing or giving away something that has a memory attached to it, keep in mind that you're only giving away the object, not the memory.

If you're worried about not remembering something, take a picture of it (the photo doesn't take up any room). The past will let go of you if you let go of the past.

Now spread your wings and fly!

Sit Happens at **TimberHawkeye.com**

If you enjoyed this book, please share it with your friends.
Sign up to receive one email from Timber each month
at TimberHawkeye.com/email

Join our online community on
Facebook and **Instagram**
@BuddhistBootCamp

Subscribe for free to the **Buddhist Boot Camp Podcast**
wherever you listen to your podcasts (iTunes, Spotify,
Google Play, Stitcher, SoundCloud, iHeartRadio, etc.)